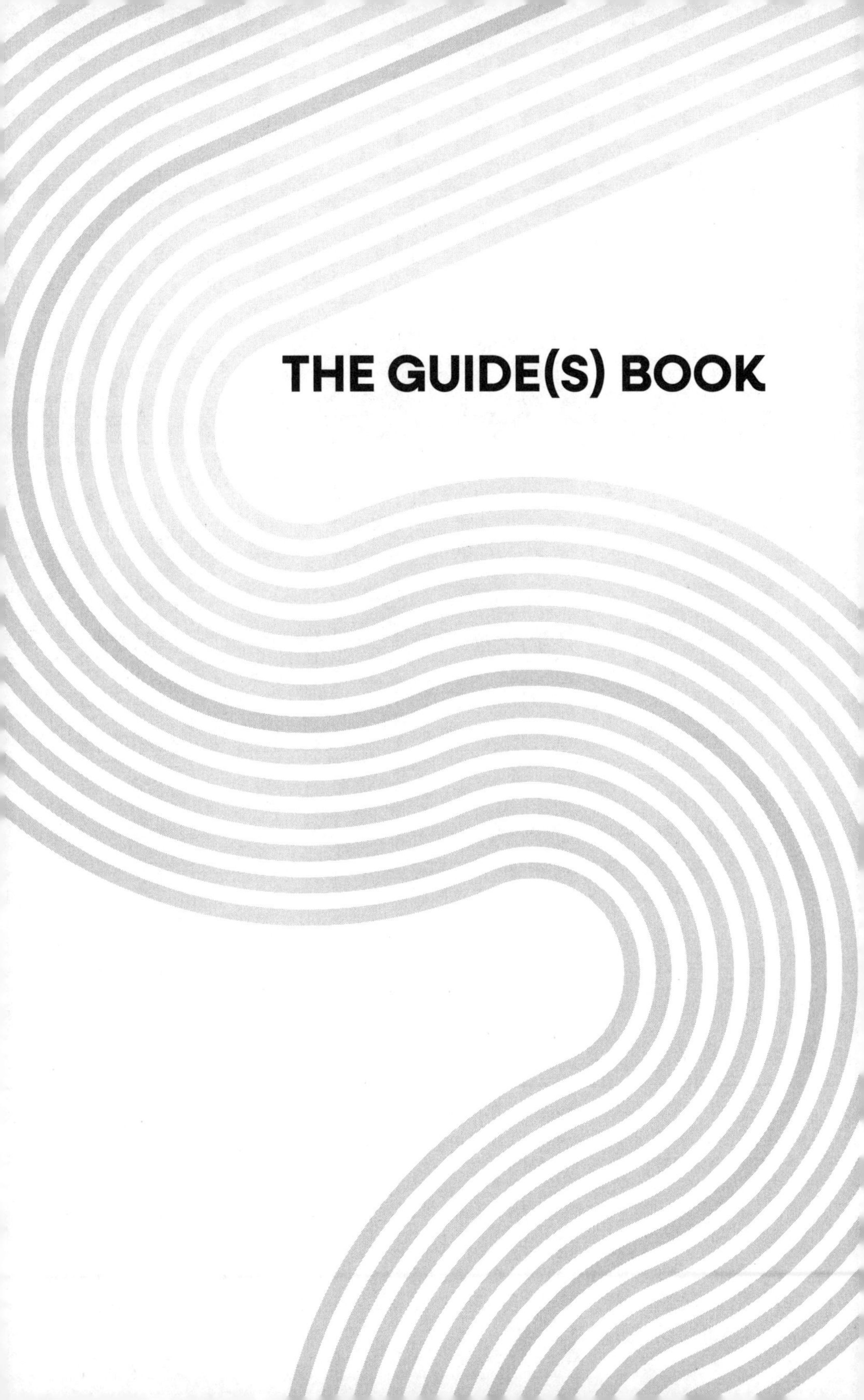

THE GUIDE(S) BOOK

THE GUIDE(S) BOOK

Mapping Out Life's Journey with Spirit by Your Side

MARYANN DIMARCO

with **CHANDIKA**

Foreword by Gabrielle Bernstein

RUNNING PRESS
PHILADELPHIA

Running Press
Hachette Book Group
1290 Avenue of the Americas, New York, NY 10104
www.runningpress.com
@Running_Press

First Edition: September 2025

Published by Running Press, an imprint of Hachette Book Group, Inc.
The Running Press name and logo are trademarks of Hachette Book Group, Inc.

Print book cover and interior design by Susan Van Horn

Library of Congress Cataloging-in-Publication Data has been applied for.

ISBNs: 979-8-89414-032-2 (hardcover), 979-8-89414-033-9 (ebook)

Printed in the United States of America

LSC-C

Printing 1, 2025

To my Spirit Guides and Source,
with gratitude for everything and then some.

CONTENTS

FOREWORD

For the past twenty years, I've worked as a spiritual teacher, offering people hope and faith in a divine connection beyond what they can see. For much of that period, I hesitated to speak openly about my full spiritual beliefs—particularly my deep knowing that we have an ever-present team of Guides supporting us at all times.

As time went on, I grew more confident in sharing my faith in Spirit Guides and their powerful presence in my life. To my surprise, this openness was met with enthusiasm. My readers and audience wanted to know more—they were eager to learn how to connect with these divine beings of light.

Enter my dear friend, MaryAnn DiMarco.

To help people deepen their connection to their Guides, I began inviting MaryAnn onto my podcast ***Dear Gabby***. Every episode with her was a hit! It was clear that people were hungry to understand their own Guides, how to connect with them, and how to receive their support.

MaryAnn's wisdom and unwavering faith in the spiritual realm are contagious. As a renowned psychic medium, she shares how her Guides have helped her make pivotal decisions, overcome self-doubt, and find meaning during difficult times. Their wise counsel acts as a compass, helping us navigate life's unpredictable path.

While MaryAnn's journey as a medium is unique, the presence of Spirit Guides is universal. She explains that each of us has a team of Spirit Guides eager to support our personal growth. By building a relationship with them, we gain access to an invaluable source of higher wisdom.

In each chapter, MaryAnn offers practical exercises to help readers strengthen their intuitive abilities. Through simple meditations and activities, we can learn to tune in to guidance—whether it comes as a gut feeling, a symbolic message, or a sudden flash of inspiration. As we refine our ability to listen, our lives take on new direction and purpose.

Life is a journey filled with twists, turns, ups, and downs. As we navigate our path, it's comforting to know we're never alone—that we are always guided. The book offers you that comfort by introducing you to your own team of Spirit Guides who are always by your side, offering direction whenever you need it. MaryAnn will teach you how everyday moments contain signs meant to guide you toward your highest self.

By bringing Spirit into our daily lives, she empowers us to live with confidence, resilience, and an open heart. She reminds us that we're not here to seek perfection, but to embrace the messy, beautiful humanity that makes our journey meaningful. Even our challenges become opportunities when we view them as lessons for the soul.

With grace and humor, MaryAnn inspires us to find beauty in the unexpected. When we approach life with an open heart and a willingness to trust our Guides, the path before us becomes joyful; we can effortlessly manifest; and most importantly we feel safe inside. May this book open your heart to a world of spiritual support, protection, and divine guidance.

—Gabrielle Bernstein

INTRODUCTION
PACKED AND READY TO GO!

About a year ago, my Guides started nagging at me to write another book. It happened the way it usually happens: ***Write a book***, they said. I flicked the thought away like a fly that had landed on my shoulder. Then a week later, the fly landed again, this time on my face: ***No, seriously. Write a book.*** I shook my head—shoo, fly! It just came back again and again, louder and louder each time until the fly was buzzing and buzzing around my head and I couldn't ignore it anymore.

"OK, fine!" I answered, with the fly now perched on the end of my nose and staring me in the face. "What do you want me to write about?"

Us.

I thought about reasoning with them. Other psychic mediums have written about Guides before, so why should I? And anyway, I *have* written about Guides before—they've had featured roles in both of my previous books. But I know that Guides aren't meant to be reasoned with, any more than they are meant to be flicked away. I accepted that I would have to write the book. I also accepted what I know to be true about writing a book: soon enough, the exact imagery I needed to frame my stories would arise, as would the stories themselves and the lessons behind them. (If you're wondering what, exactly, *Guides* are, don't fret! We'll get there shortly in chapter 1.)

What I didn't know at the outset was that the lessons would come through during a time of such challenge for me. The period during which I have written this book has been one of the most challenging periods of my life.

I want to be clear right up front with you: the challenges I've come up against in this lifetime may not seem big from your perspective. In many ways, I've been fortunate; I haven't faced a terrible diagnosis or had to deal with institutional discrimination, and though I've lost and grieved in ways that are profound to me, I haven't gone through some rare personal tragedy of the type that makes the evening news. And yet, the trajectory of my life has forced me to come up against the exact themes of my youth in new ways as an adult. Though these events may appear unremarkable from an outside perspective, for me, they are the great hurdles my soul came here to overcome. They've brought my shadow into the light, created aversions and negativity, and even left me with a lingering sense of existential dread. I've had to grieve dreams that didn't come true and remake my image of myself multiple times. I've needed my Guides to keep me from spiraling into darkness and show me the greater spiritual context for the lessons I've learned.

Your own personal challenges, however big or small they are or may appear to anyone else, are bringing you through the same process. And since one of the main functions of our Guides is to help us frame our challenges within the context of our own soul's journey, examining what pushes us to and beyond our edge is an excellent way to learn to work with the guidance available to us.

And since one of the main functions of our Guides is to help us frame our challenges within the context of our own soul's journey, examining what pushes us to and beyond our edge is an excellent way to learn to work with the guidance available to us.

NAVIGATING LIFE'S CHALLENGES

So what specific challenges am I facing in this phase of my life? Ugh! It's embarrassing to even tell you, but I know I have to so here you go:

First, once our kids grew up, my loving husband and I found ourselves living in a now-oversized family house that is no longer practical or tenable for our lives, so we decided to downsize by selling the home where we'd spent over a decade. This has also prompted us to uproot from our life on Long Island, where I'd been my entire life, and move to Florida, where we are building our next house. On top of that, we didn't realize the build would continue after we had sold our Long Island house, leaving a gap of more than a year between homes, which we are filling with rentals. This move has been 100 percent voluntary, and yet moving at all is my worst nightmare. Living in a temporary home brings up all sorts of fears and activates long-held ideas about myself and my life. Yet the more uncomfortable I've become, the more certain I am that this is the area where I am meant to do my personal work. My Guides are leading me far outside my comfort zone because there's something for me to learn.

Second, while I was writing this book, I had to put down my beloved golden retriever Phoenix. I've had many wonderful pets over the years, but Phoenix was special. The lead-up to his death was compounded by our need to sell our house—the only home he'd ever known. I started grieving long before he died and, since his passage, have mourned him as much as I've mourned some people. I've also had several friends die in the past year or two—so, as is often the case with grief, it feels like everything is mushed together. I know no one is ever gone, but I miss the earthly presence of these friends—both human and canine—and have had to deal with some big feelings around their loss.

And third, like all women who are lucky enough to live this long, I have reached the glorious change *of life, the next great shift of womanhood: menopause. (Can you hear my resistance?) This unfamiliar, bloated, confusing, emotional, and generally sweaty experience—a second puberty of sorts—has been rough on my body. It has also been rough on my self-image, much of which crystallized during and just after my first puberty (you know, puberty-puberty) oh-so-many years ago. I really haven't had to revisit much of this stuff in a long time, and it turns out, I had a lot wrapped up in it. In other words, according to my Guides, I've got a lot to unravel. At the same time, menopause is teaching me enormous amounts about myself and how I want to relate to the world around me. It's shifting my priorities, helping me with the ongoing process of moving away from people-pleasing and toward my authentic truth. I'm having about as easy a time balancing the positives and negatives of menopause as my hormones are having balancing themselves in my body—in other words, not easy at all—and I'm very much still in the thick of it. So I present to you this beloved but equally powerful mess that I call midlife.*

All of these experiences have left me navigating uncertain ground. I have had moments with the impression that I don't know who or what I am. And yet, deep down, in the middle of all this change, there are parts of me that are utterly stable and secure. I've had to lean into that truth, even as I explore parts unknown. I'm on a journey I've never been on before, so I'm choosing to see it as an adventure. It's an opportunity to embrace each moment and the lessons it contains—lessons my Guides are urging me to see at every turn.

THE BIGGEST ROAD TRIP

As I approached writing about these experiences, I asked my Guides for some imagery to help bring you, my dear reader, through this book. They immediately called out, *Road trip!* And I knew they were right (of course they were) because here's the truth: by making all this change into an adventure, I'm finding space to walk into the unknown with some semblance of grace. I'm not alone in that. Each one of you reading this book is going through life without knowing what's coming next, whether you like it or not. You're faced with a host of decisions—turn left or turn right? stop here or stop there?—as your soul progresses through its incarnation. It's best to see that process as an adventure, an experience, a (I'm so sorry to say it!) *journey* and not a destination.

It helps to look at life that way because that's how our Guides look at it. The truth is that our Guides just don't really care if we go left or right, if we make a pit stop at this gas station or the next; they know we're all getting where we're going and that we'll be provided the exact lessons we need at every turn regardless of exactly which choices we make. This book is aimed at helping you navigate your life with the best GPS possible—all directions provided by your own intuition and the guidance it connects you to.

The road each of us takes is governed in part by who we are as individuals. Each of us was gifted with a unique set of tools to understand the lessons we set out to learn in this lifetime. Those tools include our ego, that sneaky part of us that says we are separate from the collective; our innate fears, which often turn into aversions over time; our natural talents and interests, however we may have nurtured or not nurtured them; the people we have known, such as family and friends, especially early in life; and the challenges and/or traumas we have faced as a result of all of the above.

As we work toward a guided life (aka one informed by the wisdom of our team of Guides), it's important to avoid ***spiritual bypassing***. This buzzy term refers to the hope, or even expectation, that so many of us carry: that living a spiritual life is going to somehow save us from experiencing challenges here on earth. Spirituality is often sold as a solution to life itself. This does all of us a disservice, because the reality will always be that life keeps on happening. Many of us want to believe we can "take the high road" by spiritualizing our way out of everything and anything that comes our way. Yet even the most spiritual among us is not exempt from life itself.

As we work toward a guided life (aka one informed by the wisdom of our team of Guides), it's important to avoid *spiritual bypassing*. This buzzy term refers to the hope, or even expectation, that so many of us carry: that living a spiritual life is going to somehow save us from experiencing challenges here on earth.

Life is about learning, and learning is all about alchemizing our very real struggles into spiritual gold. Confronting something difficult, attempting to resolve it with an old response, failing, and finding a new response, form the process by which we grow. That doesn't mean that everything is awful all the time—some challenges are super-difficult, yes, but other, lighter challenges can be somewhat fun. They're practice!

To get good at something, we have to learn a new set of skills and then repeat them over and over. That means that even once we've learned to deal with something, the same issue is going to show up again. This is even true of our spiritual skill set. So when life hands us challenges we don't yet know how to face, we can say, "Thank you!" And when life hands us that same challenge again, we can repeat our thanks, whether it flows naturally or comes through gritted teeth. Eventually we will learn to drop our resistance and realize that our personal troubles point directly to the lessons our souls came here to learn. Our challenges are a road map, showing us how our soul is meant to progress.

Our challenges are a road map, showing us how our soul is meant to progress.

Even if our challenges aren't externally all that big, they're going to feel big to us. We're going to have to confront them, and we're going to learn a ton in the process, uncomfortable as it may be. That's the human experience: it's a big adventure, an ongoing journey, a road trip that never ends. And since our Guides are along for the ride anyway, why not start a dialogue?

Contrary to popular belief, our Guides aren't here to bring us out of all of that. It isn't their role to solve our issues and make things easy on us or to cocoon us in bubble wrap so we aren't hurt by the natural ups and downs—some of them really, really down—that come with human life. If that were the point, we simply wouldn't have challenges at all. Our Guides' role is to direct us to the lessons along the way so we don't miss what Spirit is trying to show us. Those lessons are all based on truths we already know—they're encoded on our soul—but have forgotten as part of the human experience. It's easy to get lost in the surface-level version of what's happening. Our Guides are here to bring us deeper, to help us understand how to ground the superficial events into our greater spiritual evolution.

That may bum you out a bit. You may think, ***Come on, MaryAnn, I want to get past all this human stuff! I don't want to feel pain or face loss; I don't want to grieve or have my heart break.*** I hear you, I really do. I won't be the first to respond that this is a realm of contrasts and that the sour and spicy stuff makes the sweet even sweeter. But beyond that, what would be the point of life without all that "human stuff"? Eventually, we all arrive at life, at love, at Source. (By the way, I'll use Source or Spirit throughout this text to refer to the embodiment of a higher power within myself—an idea that many people refer to by other names, such as God.) Would you really want to just show up at the last stop on the road trip, order all the souvenirs and have them delivered to the hotel, and then photoshop yourself into all the pictures? Doing that would miss the point entirely.

Seeing life's progress as a journey is hard sometimes. We live in a society that emphasizes things like immediate gratification, achievement, accomplishment, and finishing one task so we can move on to the next. But that just isn't what life is about. We're here to learn, and to do that, we sometimes have to struggle a bit. The hardest-won lessons are the best ones. They all contribute to our soul's ascension.

With that in mind, let's consider my role in this process, as your very fallible, very human guide along the way. I want to be clear up front about how I can help as well as how I can't.

I'M NOT YOUR MAGIC 8 BALL

You may be too young to remember the actual physical Magic 8 Balls, but in the 1970s and '80s when I was growing up, it seemed like they were *everywhere*. Magic 8 Balls were these big plastic toys, painted like the number 8 black-and-white billiard ball, that you needed to hold and shake with two hands. You shook them because they contained a twenty-sided die hanging out in this murky liquid, and eventually one of the sides of that die would rise up to a little window and provide fortune-cookie-esque wisdom such as "Signs point to yes" or "Ask again later." You'd ask the Magic 8 Ball questions—mostly about romance and other teenage problems, let's be honest—and it would answer them. (Then if you didn't like the answer, you'd just ask and shake again—we can be honest about that part, too.)

As soon as I started putting myself out into the world as a psychic medium over a decade ago, I started to notice that people wanted to use me like a Magic 8 Ball. They'd pepper me with questions and listen to the answers. I decided to go professional, and that worked, because there was never a shortage of people asking questions or appreciating the answers. It also worked because I was (and am) pretty good at it—I'm a bona fide psychic medium who has worked hard to hone my psychic skills, so the answers I provide are true and real. Yet just being in this role bothered me. It didn't feel like enough to just *answer* questions; I was being called to teach people how to answer them *on their own*.

I cataloged my early experiences as a psychic medium in my first book *Believe, Ask, Act.* Then, several years ago, I began to mentor developing psychics and psychic mediums. (By the way, a ***psychic*** is someone who has honed their intuition, and a ***psychic medium*** is someone whose intuition allows them to speak with loved ones who have crossed over.) I began to collect these experiences to put toward my next book *Medium Mentor.* Both books tell stories from my life while helping others realize their own psychic gifts.

In that regard, this book is no different: it tells stories from my life and those of my clients and students (most of whose names and personal information have been changed to protect identities) while helping you realize that you, too, have a very strong inner compass you can access anytime. It encourages you—ahem, *strongly*—to stay grounded, to not let the woo whisk you away into the ethers, but rather to keep your two feet on the ground as you bring this work into your life, right here, right now. I've ended each chapter with an experiential exercise that you're welcome to adapt however you need to and use as many times as you want. The tools in this book are only practical if they're practiced, so regardless of how you shift them for your needs and your situation, I highly recommend giving these exercises a try.

How is this book different from the others? I'm taking you to new places by focusing even more deeply on helping you access the voice of your Spirit Guides—in your way and on your schedule. This is an integral part of any intuitive's experience.

I'm also road-tripping through entirely new territory for me, pushing myself to the limit by telling quite a few of my own stories from this rather challenging era of my life. I'm diving deep, getting personal. I'm revealing parts of myself that aren't always so fun to look at: my vanity, my avoidance, the things that have brought me to my knees. Behind every personal challenge is some sort of pain. My hope is that by sharing that pain, I can knock myself off any pedestal you might be tempted to put me on. I'm a spiritualist, not a saint. I can shut down, withdraw, get angry, and hide. Being a teacher and author in the spiritual arena doesn't exempt me from that. I am lucky, though, in that I look at things a little bit differently—this is an analytical lifetime for me, one during which I'm more curious about what challenges me than I am troubled by it. Yet I want to show you that I, too, have a shadow. In doing so, I'm straying a little bit outside my comfort zone and hoping you can do the same. We both know that it's in this exciting, slightly terrifying space that transformation occurs.

Through this journey that we take together, you won't just understand who your Spirit Guides are and how to work with them. You're also going to unveil who you can be when you connect with them on a regular basis. You'll discover how, with your Spirit Guides at your side, you can approach your life with curiosity about the greater lessons it has to teach you. You'll find yourself navigating your days with the confidence, curiosity, and enthusiasm you may have looked to others to provide you in the past. Instead of reaching outward for that Magic 8 Ball, you'll reach inward to find the answers that are just hanging out, waiting to rise to the surface.

Through this journey that we take together, you won't just understand who your Spirit Guides are and how to work with them. You're also going to unveil who you can be when you connect with them on a regular basis. You'll discover how, with your Spirit Guides at your side, you can approach your life with curiosity about the greater lessons it has to teach you. You'll find yourself navigating your days with the confidence, curiosity, and enthusiasm you may have looked to others to provide you in the past. Instead of reaching outward for that Magic 8 Ball, you'll reach inward to find the answers that are just hanging out, waiting to rise to the surface.

Ready? Grab your bags! It's time to hit the road.

Chapter 1
YOUR SPIRITUAL RIDE OR DIE

WORKING WITH GUIDES IS A LIFELONG PROCESS THAT BRINGS infinite comfort and direction to our lives. Throughout this book, I'll offer tips and tricks to help you hear the guidance that has always been available to you—the messages that are meant just for you, to push your individual soul along in its development. But first, let's start with the basics. Why do we need Spirit Guides? What are they doing? And most importantly: what are Spirit Guides in the first place?

What Are Spirit Guides?

Each week, I'm asked the same question by my students: who and what are Spirit Guides anyway?

The answer isn't complicated. Spirit Guides are a Universal Team of lightworkers assigned to navigate us through this crazy thing we call life. They are disembodied beings who aren't presently walking on this planet as we do, but who can influence our earthly events just the same. They do that by guiding us through the options of which way to go, showing us how to hear our true inner knowing, and uncovering the higher lessons we came here to learn in the process. Spirit Guides are the means by which we connect to Source. They are, in essence, an intermediary between humans and the divine, who can put Source energy into words, images, and ideas we can understand.

Spirit Guides are a Universal Team of lightworkers assigned to navigate us through this crazy thing we call life. They are disembodied beings who aren't presently walking on this planet as we do, but who can influence our earthly events just the same. They do that by guiding us through the options of which way to go, showing us how to hear our true inner knowing, and uncovering the higher lessons we came here to learn in the process. Spirit Guides are the means by which we connect to Source. They are, in essence, an intermediary between humans and the divine, who can put Source energy into words, images, and ideas we can understand.

As a medium, I channel messages from Spirit Guides all the time—my own, of course, and the Guides of the brave and curious seekers who ask for my help. I also channel other beings, like loved ones and angels. While these beings are all part of our Spiritual Universal Team, for this book and teaching purposes, it is important that I distinguish the difference in the roles they play in our lives.

Loved ones are the people we have known in this lifetime who have passed on. They once had bodies—and in most cases will again—but in the space between lifetimes they come to us to reassure us that there is more than just this body, that the Universe is far greater than the world we can see and touch. Sometimes they'll come in to shed light on a situation, but the guidance they provide is more general than the advice Spirit Guides give. I often channel them as saying things like, *All will be well,* or *There's no need to worry,* or *I am with you.* They often comment on what an individual already knows, confirming what we suspect to be the case. This is often a highly emotional experience. When loved ones give direct messages, they are usually doing so based on what they learned in their own life or at the moment of death, as well as what that represents to us.

For instance, my friend Anne Marie was always really conscious of her body. She looked great, but she was hard on herself when she ate something she felt she shouldn't have or when she had a bad hair day. We'd often connect on these issues, chiding ourselves for skipping a workout at the gym or curling up on the couch late at night with a sleeve of Oreos. After Anne Marie died and became one of my loved ones on the Other Side, I had a profound dream about her in which we were going to a party, dressed to the nines. She turned and looked at me and said, "MaryAnn, eat all the Thanksgiving dinner—and then some." It was a completely uncharacteristic thing for her to say, but she delivered it with that same Anne Marie wit I would recognize anywhere! I woke up knowing that after her death, as Anne Marie's soul made sense of the events of her life, she had come to appreciate everyday experiences in a new way—what the Italians call *dolce far niente*, or the simple sweetness of doing nothing at all. She wanted me to learn to release the habit of judging my body while I was still alive, because it was holding me back from the sweetness still available to me. This is the kind of guidance loved ones give; it's more about our inner experience, and less about what, specifically, we're meant to do or say as we move through the world. (Don't worry—if you want more on that, there's a lot more on loved ones in chapter 4.)

Unlike loved ones, angels appear to me as bodies of light and are only sometimes visible. They're not as dense as us, but they are much more powerful. Those who have seen angels will tell you: they're *huge*! These enormous spirits have ascended to a higher plane of consciousness and yet they watch over us here on earth, offering protection so that we can keep learning the lessons we came here to experience. Angels often appear to perform protective miracles; people experience them at accident scenes, in hospital rooms, or in moments of great fear. While only some people will be lucky enough to see their angels, everyone has them, just as everyone has Spirit Guides and loved ones watching over their lives. For those who are drawn to angels, I highly recommend Kyle Gray's books and decks.

Some people work with archangels, as well, such as Michael or Raphael. These archangels have a protective energy, but theirs tends to focus on specific areas of life. They don't provide the same sort of direction as Spirit Guides, either; they are helpful in other ways. But in some circumstances, angels can be similar; we can pull a card from an angel deck and receive guidance, no problem.

In other words, angels protect us, loved ones reassure us, and Spirit Guides show us the way. Spirit Guides may provide some of the things loved ones and angels do, such as reassuring us, ***You've got this!*** or moving us away from situations that might harm us. But above all, Spirit Guides are directive. They offer instructions that go beyond the purview of angels and loved ones.

Spirit Guides always have a shared singular goal behind their instructions: to guide us toward the lessons we're here to learn and the higher knowing that underpins them all. Our highest being—that deep sense of certainty in the core of our selves—knows what's right for us, but it can be easy to forget. The goal of Spirit Guides is to help us remember. This is why our Spirit Guides are our very best friends. It's essential that we befriend our Spirit Guides, understanding their vital role in our human experience. And the process starts with recognizing they've already befriended us! They know everything about us—our hopes, our fears, our flaws, our secrets. It may be that they knew all of this before you were even born. And still, they love you and are cheering you along, flaws and all. They are, quite literally, part of your team. Treat them as such! Be informal, be comfortable, be forward with your requests. Know deep in your heart that ***you can't do this wrong***. Getting that point clear at the outset will enhance the entire process of connecting to and working with your Guides.

And don't forget—Guides *love* gratitude! Show them gratitude as often as you can—not because anything will go wrong if you don't, but simply because they enjoy it when you do.

The first time I connected with one of my Spirit Guides, I was going through a very tough time in my life. I was in the midst of a rebirth. I had been called by Spirit, and though I was in the middle of a divorce that in many ways smashed my false sense of identity to pieces, the experience allowed me to become who I really am. I had been a stay-at-home mom while my kids were young, but by then they had entered school, and while much of my life still revolved around taking them to their activities, preparing after-school snacks, helping them with homework, and even acting as an appointed member of the school board, I had just enough free time to start thinking about myself and my own needs again for the first time in years. It occurred to me that I wanted to start working again—also, after my first husband and I separated, I needed to find a way to support myself—but I didn't want to go back to the career I'd had before. I had no idea which direction to choose.

At the same time, I was also embracing my identity as a medium and had begun training under teacher Pat Longo. Mediumship had been in my sphere for a long time, as I described in my first book *Believe, Ask, Act*. My mother had taught me to meditate when I was young, as she subscribed to many New Age ideas—I come from a long line of women who were open to their psychic gifts and have always been drawn toward psychic mediums for readings. But I wanted to be "normal" (whatever that means!). I didn't want to draw negative attention to myself, which coming out of the spiritual closet in many social circles tends to do. So even though I still had no sense this would become a career for me, the very fact that I was taking classes in mediumship challenged me on a whole new level. It wasn't something I thought my regular suburban churchgoing mom-life could support. At the time, I worried that developing my spiritual gifts would alienate me from the only world I knew.

One night I was lying in my bed when I suddenly noticed a little bit of light coming through the window, casting a shadow on the wall—one that couldn't have been cast by any physical objects in the room. It appeared to be a sort of ancient Egyptian–looking head and headdress. (You may be thinking, *Ancient Egypt?!* How does that match up with an Italian American from Long Island? I know, I know—I wondered about that, too! Keep reading, because there's more on the multicultural nature of Spirit Guides in chapter 2.) I've always loved ancient Egyptian culture, and seeing this immediately recalled the afterlife and the ornate rituals of preparing loved ones for what comes for them after death. At first, I just thought it looked interesting, but then I found myself focusing more and more deeply on the shadow, going into a sort of trancelike state as I did.

Through *claircognizance*, or spiritual knowing, I understood that a message was coming through for me about engaging in spiritual communication on behalf of others. Then I heard a voice talking to me, explaining that part of my mission in this life was to teach others about Spirit, spiritual guidance, and the afterlife. I realized I had done similar work in the past and understood that I experienced at least one past life in ancient Egypt, where there was a common cultural understanding of the afterlife—in fact, it was my experiences there that had drawn me toward ancient Egyptian imagery and rituals my whole life. The Guide communicated to me that he was there to increase or open my abilities of spiritual communication. The entire interaction couldn't have been more than a few minutes, but when I trusted what I heard, it instantaneously sharpened my spiritual senses, or *clairs*.

Not too long after that, in one of Pat's classes, she asked me to "read the group." That meant I was supposed to look around the circle of students until I felt Spirit pulling me toward a certain person and then start channeling for them. I'd usually channel loved ones who had passed over, but not this time. Instead, I found myself looking at one of my classmates and not understanding what I was experiencing—the energy seemed entirely different from a loved one. What began to come through didn't feel like somebody my classmate had known personally in life; instead, in my third eye I began to visualize a very angelic-looking figure surrounded by a diverse crowd of human and humanlike individuals. That's when I heard, *You're seeing her Guide.* I delivered the message the Guide gave me and turned to the next person in the circle, because I saw an energy next to her, and began to channel that Guide. The other students got really excited! I went around the room and, one by one, I channeled a Guide for each of the other students. Pat just sat there smiling.

Since that day, I've learned to work with Spirit Guides in a variety of other ways, too. As intermediaries, Spirit Guides give us the direction we need to make the highest and best choices for ourselves and others. They're looking out for us, but they're also looking out for everyone else—their direction is for the good of all. It's their job to channel Source energy, helping us to make sense of what Spirit (or God or a Higher Power or the Universe) wants for us. Spirit is the concentrated intention of Source energy. Yet a part of Spirit lives in each one of us—it's our very highest self. That means that when we're communicating with our Spirit Guides, we're simultaneously communicating with Spirit, Source, and self. Our Guides are showing us how to access our own highest knowing, channeling from and with love and light.

On a practical level, Spirit Guides can help us make life decisions, like *What is this relationship trying to show me?* or *How can I make the best of a difficult event?* They can also help us make small, everyday decisions, like *Which of these two specialists should I see?* or *Is this house the right one for me?* When we tap into the power of our Spirit Guides, we can navigate life with greater ease. We can know, deep down in our belly, that we aren't alone. This knowledge doesn't take away our challenges—life is all about challenges, even for psychic mediums!—but it helps us work our way through them in a way that feels hopeful and supported.

Our Spirit Guides are there whether we choose to work with them or not. So, then, what are the benefits of looking to them for support?

Why We Need Them

The main reason to work with our Spirit Guides is that doing so raises our vibration. It puts our focus where it matters most: on the unseen aspects of life, the magical realm that governs all that happens here on earth. We are all being guided, whether we choose to believe it or not. You deciding to read this book is a perfect example of Guides giving direction. *Hey, you've been wanting to know how to connect with your Guides. Look here, this is the perfect book. Go ahead and put that in your cart.* You could have ignored that direction, but you didn't! You listened and you said yes. Well done!

And we need their guidance. By pointing us in the right direction, our Spirit Guides help us navigate our own lives in the way that only we can. Spirit speaks to us by sending life events our way for us to interpret as part of the greater lessons we are learning in this lifetime. Our Guides, then, point us toward this interpretation, helping us make sense of what is happening so we can use it for our own evolution.

I am currently passing though one of the more challenging periods in my life. But it does not exist in a vacuum from the rest of my life's journey. The sense of panic I feel around selling one house and building another has deep roots.

My parents' divorce was the first time I went through significant life-changing challenge. Years before it happened, I had had a terrifying dream I later came to see as prophetic. My family was traveling in our old brown

Buick. My father was driving; my mother was in the passenger seat; and my brother and I were seated behind them. We drove toward a dock at the marina near our house on Long Island. I stared out the thick back window at the water and the boats dotting the landscape, my wide eyes and Toni Tenille haircut reflecting in the glass. It wasn't until I felt the wheels bumping across uneven planks that I realized we were on the dock itself, still going some thirty miles per hour as if my father had no intention of stopping. This seemed wrong somehow, but my mother and brother stared straight forward unconcerned. Before I could shout, "No!" my father lost control and the entire car launched off the dock and sank down into the bay. The frigid cold water came streaming in from all sides. I felt myself lifting up off the seat until my head hit the ceiling, watching my mother and brother and father around me. There we were: all four of us pressed flat against the ceiling, kicking against the tan interior and each other as we pounded our fists against the windows. Water entered my nose and throat, and my eyes refused to close on my family as I choked. We were drowning like that when I woke up.

This dream, I later understood, was trying to show me what I would experience emotionally some years later during and after my parents' divorce. It was showing me that I wasn't feeling those feelings accidentally; I was having them because they held the richest lessons for me, some of the most important lessons I came here to encounter.

Each of us arrives in this lifetime with lessons to learn. Our entire lives—the events that take place, people we encounter, choices we make—are set up to help us learn those lessons. Our highest being knows this and is not afraid of what we might face as part of that learning. Our ego, on the other hand, is terrified. The role of our Spirit Guides is to shepherd us through our fear and back toward the lessons our lives are trying to teach us.

The role of our Spirit Guides is to shepherd us through our fear and back toward the lessons our lives are trying to teach us.

My dear friend Gabrielle Bernstein, who is a best-selling author and spiritual teacher, had a chance to relearn this during her fertility journey (a deeply personal topic that she has shared about extensively through her blog posts, videos, live talks, and books). It took her three years to conceive her son. Gabby is one of the most positive people I know. It seems like her faith never wavers: she maintains an unflappable belief in her power to manifest and is always reminding me that "rejection is protection." But doubt and fear are common issues for women on a fertility journey, and she understood that if she gave into them it would be impossible to manifest the child she dreamed of having. So even though she felt fear, she understood that the Universe wasn't rejecting her desire to have a child. Instead, her Guides were trying to show her the next steps for her soul's progression—steps that needed to happen *before* she could become a mother.

Gabby and I had some deep talks during that time—some when I acted as a mentor and many more where I was just a friend who heard her out and offered comfort. Gabby first addressed her need to control the timeline and the outcome. (Keep reading—timeline and outcome will come up a lot in the pages to come!) Then, she took a yearlong break from trying to conceive while she worked with doctors on her gut health. She knew that while she dealt with the physical realities that were preventing her from conceiving, she also needed to keep her vibration high. To hold doubt and fear at bay, Gabby regularly asked for signs to remind her that her Guides were at her side. She initially asked to see owls, and of course she started seeing and hearing owls everywhere. (What can I say, she's an amazing manifestor!)

Then, though she hadn't asked for lilies as a sign, they started to show up for her as well. I even started seeing lilies for Gabby! One day we were chatting as I was driving, and I saw the word *lily* on the side of a truck. Soon after that, Gabby found out that lilies are the sign of Archangel Gabriel, the angel assigned to helping with fertility and maternity. Lilies were appearing to remind Gabby that Gabriel was a Guide for her during this difficult period.

One night I was channeling for Gabby over the phone, and right then, I looked over and saw that the Easter lily in my house had bloomed! It was the first time it had ever bloomed, so it was really a surprise. I started telling her about it, and just then, I heard an owl hooting outside. We were both excited because we knew her Guides were there to quiet her doubts and calm her fear.

For her, the process was largely about learning to trust. She had a relationship with her Guides before her fertility journey, but the bond grew so much in those years as she learned to rely on her intuition, her knowing, and her Guides' greater plan for her. The result? Three years after she first started trying, Gabby conceived her dear son Oliver, little Ollie, who is as delightful as can be.

How Our Guides Work

As Gabby's story shows, our Guides work through signs, symbols, roadblocks—you name it! That said, they don't work alone. It's our job to interpret what our Guides are communicating to us and put it into action.

That brings me to one of the main points of this book—and indeed of all my work as an author and teacher: it's up to you to do the work. Your Spirit Guides aren't going to fix your problems. They aren't going to give your life a makeover so your troubles go away and everything is shiny and new. Instead, they're going to show *you* how to do those things. And then, its going to be up to you to do them.

Take my student Sam as an example. Sam was working on discerning the voice of his Spirit Guides so he could make life decisions with their help. In the late 2010s, Sam started looking for a new place to live. He was working in LA, where he had lived for years, and had no intention of moving—he just needed a new house. Try as he might, he couldn't find the right one. Everything that seemed almost-right fell through. Time and again, Sam would find himself outbid or would realize something wasn't right with a house or would get caught up in bureaucracy and back off. What was going on? It was as if his Guides simply didn't want him to buy property in LA.

Instead, the Guides were clear about what was going on: *Move back to Tucson,* they said. Tucson?! Sam was annoyed. He'd grown up there and enjoyed going back to visit his parents, but his life, his friends, and his job were all in LA. It took quite a while, but eventually Sam listened and uprooted his California life to move back to his home state. His company transferred him to its Phoenix office, which was more of a commute than he liked but still possible, and he spent much of his first few months with his parents, since they were finally close to him after decades spent apart.

That was late in 2019. By March 2020, Sam's move finally made sense: the COVID-19 pandemic was in full swing. He brought his parents groceries and no longer even had to deal with the commute when his job went remote. That summer, his mother contracted the coronavirus and died not long after. Sam was so grateful to have been able to spend those last few months with her. It was also a huge help to his father having him around; they could grieve together and support each other through the adjustment. Though Sam couldn't have predicted the pandemic, it appeared that his Guides had and put him exactly where he needed to be for the final months of his mother's life.

Sam's Guides showed him which way to go by putting up roadblocks in LA and whispering in his ear about Tucson. But it was up to him to make the moves and take the actions. The same will be true for you as you connect with your Guides through this book: they'll indicate which way to go, but you'll need to act on the directions you hear.

As disembodied beings, our Guides get a whole lot of pleasure out of watching us succeed. They want to see us access our highest selves and act with confidence as we spread our light through the world. I believe it's joyful for them, even fun!

As you can see through Sam's and Gabby's stories, Spirit Guides often block our ability to manifest what we *think* we want to help us receive something that is even greater for us. My own divorce, as dismantling as it was for me, pushed me so far toward my edge that I began mediumship training. If I had manifested the marriage I wanted and stayed in it, I honestly don't know if I ever would have pursued classes with Pat. So my Guides putting up a roadblock there showed me I had to leave a situation that, from the outside, seemed comfortable.

It was the right thing for me, and looking back, I see that clearly. It was part of a lesson that my higher self designed. And in the end, that's our Guides' main job: to help us hear our own highest self and the true story that's meant for us in the context of our soul's progression throughout many lifetimes. Like a snowflake or a fingerprint, our soul's mission is unique to us. We come here with that mission lying dormant within us. Our Guides are here to aid us in accessing our highest self, living within our highest vibration, and in doing so, see our mission clearly. When we work with them long enough, we learn that we have all the answers we need. ***You have the answer to that,*** they teach us. ***You don't have to ask us; listen to what your soul knows.***

That's part of why our Guides so often sound almost exactly like us. I often notice my students are waiting for a big booming voice, something outside of them, heard separately from themselves. I had the same experience when I first started training, as I explained in my second book *Medium Mentor.* I kept waiting for *clairaudience*—the technical term for what's happening when we receive spiritual guidance through hearing—to sound like something other than my own thoughts. Then Pat said something I will never forget: "Spirit speaks in your own voice." Suddenly, I realized that my Guides had been speaking to me all the time—I'd just been mistaking their statements for my own thoughts.

I started looking back over my life and realizing my Guides had been with me all along. Once, when I was in my early twenties, an ex-boyfriend called me out of the blue to suggest we meet up. I hadn't heard from him in years. I held the phone to my ear in shock. ***Bad news***, I heard, yet still agreed to meet him. ***Don't go***, my inner voice said, but I said I would go in the hope I could get some sort of closure. ***Don't do it***, said the Guides, as I checked myself one last time in the mirror and walked out to my car.

I settled into the driver's seat, put the key in the ignition, and turned it. The engine turned over but would not catch. I tried again, desperate, until I suddenly got the joke. I leaned my head back on the headrest and laughed.

Even though I hadn't yet met a Guide face-to-face, I knew someone was looking out for me that day. Whatever that reunion may have held, it wasn't right for me.

I started to make sense of these incidents from my past and understand that the inner knowing I'd always had *was* my guidance—it was my Spirit Guides pointing me toward my own intuition. Meanwhile, I continued to read other people's Guides through the mediumship classes I was taking. At one point I told Pat that people had started asking me for readings outside of class. Some friends had asked, too, and even friends of friends. Pat said something to the effect of "Well, of course they are—and you're going to have to charge people for those readings!" I was taken aback, because I'd never considered such a thing. But really it was a call to service: I was being asked, so I stepped up. As I started doing the readings, I realized that without even trying, I'd accidentally stumbled upon a career that could meet all my needs. I could build my own schedule and still be home for my kids most of the time. I had some income coming in while I was still learning and evolving in a way that suited my interest. It felt like I was moving forward. So even though offering private readings was way outside of my comfort zone, I did it. My job was to get out of my comfort zone, accept that on the surface I still felt like I didn't know what I was doing, and do it anyway. It was a first step in a process I'm still undergoing today: defeating impostor syndrome and seeing myself as someone who helps sustain her family.

In fact, the first step on my new professional path was not that different from what I'm still doing: just listening to my Guides and following what they tell me. At one point, one of them said I would teach others about mediumship, so eventually I started doing that. Then they told me to write a book, and another, and another. I choose to say yes. That's part of my mission, and saying yes helps support that.

More than a decade since that first Guide came to me as a shadow on the wall, I have come to know my Guides and have developed a deep trust and affection for them. Working with them consistently has allowed me to create a bonded relationship that I hold dear. They have continued to show up for me in countless ways. It doesn't mean that difficult things don't come my way—they do! After all, I've come here with my own wild set of lessons to learn. But my Guides have taught me how to cultivate a relationship that allows me to hear all my soul needs to find out, as well as what it already knows to be true. My Guides have been with me my whole life, but it wasn't until my work as a psychic medium began to grow that I understood the full nature of not only their presence, but their purpose. They're here to show me the way—just as your own Guides will show you.

As you read these words, you may have already had an experience with a Spirit Guide. Or, as is so often the case, you may ***think*** you might have but aren't sure. You may also have never met a Spirit Guide in your life! No matter your background, the following exercise will lead you straight to your very own Guide—one that is waiting for you.

EXERCISE: MEET YOUR GUIDE

For this meditation, you may choose to sit or lie down. In either case, straighten and align your spine. I suggest starting by lighting some sage or other smudging herbs (honor the origins and check your sourcing!), anointing yourself with holy water, or otherwise indicating to your Guides that you are cleansing yourself of any negative energy. Then, connect with your breath and take a moment to feel the weight of your body supported by the earth. Allow yourself to root down through your tailbone, sitz bones, feet, or anywhere else that is in contact with the ground. I recommend this basic beginning, called *cleansing and grounding*, for all the meditations in this book.

Once you feel clear of external energy and rooted into the earth, you may begin.

Imagine a long road in front of you, stretching far toward the horizon. Surrounding you is a landscape of your choice—it could be snowcapped mountains, a lake or river, a sandy shoreline, a forest, green hills, a desert in bloom, or any other natural setting that feels like home to you. See the road within that space and know that it represents your path of life here on earth.

Breathe deeply as you relax into this space. Allow your psychic senses to come alive as you feel the sun on your shoulders or the cool water against your fingers; as you listen to the birds in the trees; as you smell the fresh scent of the air, noticing if it's dry or humid, warm or cold. When you feel that your entire being is concentrated in this place, begin walking along the path toward the horizon. Feel the ground under your feet as you walk. Is the road bumpy or smooth, hard or soft? Be present with the sensations to awaken your psychic senses.

As you walk, you will notice that the scenery is becoming brighter and brighter, shifting toward a brilliant light. With each step you walk further into this amazing loving light, until you are surrounded by its magnificent beauty. Allow yourself to bathe in this light, feeling your entire body immersed within it as you merge into it. Imagine yourself stretching out your arms to welcome the light, basking in the love and wisdom held within it. Breathe there for several breaths.

As you look ahead into the bright white light, see a figure start to form. Notice that you welcome this figure with complete trust and love, as if it were a very old friend. Then allow the figure to walk toward you. You may be able to perceive colors, specific shapes, items that the figure carries with them, or even a face. Let your Spirit Guide appear to you with as much detail as they choose to share at this time.

Greet your Guide with gratitude. Say aloud, "Thank you for being here and for sharing with me what it is that I am ready to know."

Then, either out loud or silently, begin to ask your Guide what you need to know right now. Perhaps you're going through a difficult time and need some perspective. Perhaps you have to make a decision and want to hear what is best for you. Perhaps you're trying to make sense of something that happened in the past. Whatever your questions are, ask them with respect and humility, prepared to receive the answer.

Your conversation may be long or short. You will know, or your Guide will indicate, when it is complete.

Then thank your Guide for being there, either verbally or with a hug. Now that you have welcomed this Guide into your consciousness, you will likely see them again. Indicate your willingness to do so and say aloud, "I am ready to hear and receive my highest guidance."

See your Guide step backward into the bright whiteness. Experience its brilliance for a few more breaths and then allow it to start to fade. In your mind's eye, see yourself turn around and walk the path back as the landscape becomes clear once again. Breathe deeply in and out, preparing yourself to finish the meditation, and then open your eyes.

Know that you can request this Guide's presence at any time or, if you wish to see them directly again, call them back by repeating this meditation.

I highly encourage you to journal your experiences right away, including all the details you remember, before going back to your day.

Chapter 2
ROAD TRIP!

AS WE GET TO KNOW OUR GUIDES, IT'S FUN TO TRY TO IMAGINE exactly how many of them there are. Tens? Hundreds? Thousands? While meeting a Spirit Guide face-to-face is an incredible experience, many people still struggle to truly accept that we have loads of them and they are all just waiting for us to reach out and chat. Believe it. Your team contains a multitude of Guides, all here to help you do your life's work.

Some Guides work with fewer people, meaning we may be one of just a few individuals they are guiding at any point in time. Others, however, have been seen, heard, and felt by hundreds, sometimes thousands of others over the years. Spirit Guides are timeless and ageless; the same images can appear to generation after generation. Some of the most famous ones include Abraham, a collective voice most famously channeled by Esther Hicks; Thoth, the ibis-headed god from ancient Egypt; Mary Magdalene, a Catholic saint and an important figure in esoteric Christianity; Bashar, an extraterrestrial being whose best-known channeler is Darryl Anka; and Babaji, who has been seen by countless seekers throughout the generations in India.

Whether we see a well-known Guide or our own personal version, all Guides are symbolic. The form they take represents the reason they come into our lives. For instance, many people (myself included) are in touch with ancient Egyptians. That culture was bound by a strong belief in the afterlife and a deep understanding of ritual. For many, it brings to mind a mysterious wisdom, along with the gift of communication. People see ancient Egyptian Guides to remind them that the very same wisdom is available to them if they can bring ritual into their lives and lean into their understanding of life beyond death, allowing them to communicate across realms. Angels represent light and protection. They often appear to people who are overcoming a transpersonal pattern (i.e., a pattern that has lasted many lifetimes) of focusing on the dark. Angels are here to bring their souls to a lighter, higher vibration. It isn't uncommon for Spirit Guides to take a maternal form or to appear as a man with a long white beard (yes, I know him, too!). He represents wisdom and guidance related to psychic abilities and mediumistic skills. Indigenous Guides, which are common across cultures, often remind us how to ground ourselves and connect with the earth. Each of these commonly seen Guides has a role to play, which is often a direct reflection of how we experience them.

Hold on, you may think, ***aren't these all just stereotypes?*** It's awkward to say, but yes! Everything in the psychic realm comes in through our own imagination and frame of reference. Things appear to us in a way that will be easiest for us to understand. Spirit can guide us in any form, but that guidance is best received when we can make sense of it, so it comes in a manner we can wrap our mind around easily.

And since our imaginations are varied, Spirit Guides can take unique individual forms as well, often based on stories or concepts we've encountered in the past. I have heard of Merlin, fairies, gnomes, giants, and anything else that our minds can dream up! Some of these will match our own background; others, however, may be far less familiar.

Seeing Different Faces

Since our Guides often take recognizable forms from our frames of reference and they are higher beings than us, it isn't surprising to learn that many people see Guides connected to different religions. I have seen Guides from all walks of life, many of them religious and others not. When I'm working with people who have a deep faith in religion, I will often perceive them with figures of faith next to them. This includes deities of all types; Guides can derive from a wide array of religious backgrounds, such as (in no particular order) Jewish, Protestant, Buddhist, Catholic, Hindu, Muslim, or Indigenous. Our Guides want to be relatable to us, so they're going to use whatever imagery exists in our own minds to symbolically represent their role in our lives and the work they came to do with us.

This can work in two ways. If someone has a strong affinity for Catholicism, they may have a Guide that takes a nurturing, maternal role show up as Mother Mary. This person may see Mary when they are calling upon guidance in their own path as a mother or when they need to be mothered, as well as when they want to step into their divine femininity. This person probably will be unfazed to find that their Spirit Guide takes that form.

Another person may have a strong aversion to Catholicism. They may be very surprised to meet Mary in a meditation! Yet they are just as likely to encounter her but for entirely different reasons. To them, Mary may arrive when they need to open their mind, put down their defenses, or see something in a new light. The same entity can arrive to two different people with two entirely different messages, each based on their existing frame of reference and the symbolic meaning the entity has in their mind and experience.

For instance, my student Stephanie told me how she was sitting in a meditation circle when her higher self appeared to her as Kali, the Hindu goddess of death and destruction that is necessary for rebirth to take place. While she was somewhat frightened—Kali is an intensely powerful energy to encounter—she could easily welcome the symbolism into her sphere. She had not been raised with any type of religion, but since she came from a largely Judeo-Christian culture, she found the experience surprising. As she progressed along her spiritual path, she ended up going to India and working with tantric priests who repeatedly told her she was connected to Kali. She came to understand that it was this version of the divine feminine—a much rawer form uncommon within a Judeo-Christian framework—that she could connect with. She spent the next years engaged in tantric ceremonies through an Indian lineage, working with Kali frequently as her Guide.

Later she was in another group meditation, this one set to a playlist. Her mind had wandered to her experiences of past abuse from men when a new track started, chanting the names of Jesus and Mary. Then Jesus himself appeared to her, holding a sword of blue light. She came to understand that this Guide was there to show her the gentle, pure healing love that came from the softer versions of the divine and that Jesus wanted her to experience that from a male entity. She spent at least twenty minutes just bathing in the crystalline blue-tinged glow coming from Jesus's sword—the blue sword that is famously attributed to Saint Michael, the archangel of protection—before he faded away. She didn't go on to have frequent encounters with Jesus, but meeting him changed her view of Christianity forever.

When we see Guides that are from a different background or religion than our own, they are often trying to show us that there is no right or wrong belief system, as long as the information we receive is for the greater good. This type of encounter can also sometimes symbolize something we were connected with in a past life or an area about which we are curious and looking to explore. I'm never surprised when I see a religious figure standing behind someone who identifies themselves as an atheist. Often, these figures are there to remind me as I read them that a higher power exists for everyone in various forms.

This same concept applies beyond religion, as it is common to visualize Guides from a variety of cultures, points in time, and even planets. Some people are visited by celestial Guides who come from other galaxies, parts unexplored as yet by science. While it is possible to have waking visions of our Guides, they can also come through dreams.

Personally, I have had dreams about different Guides from different cultures and religious traditions—Hindu, African, Aztecs, etc. These dreams are so clear and so lucid that they are unmistakable to me: I know I am being asked to expand my mind and learn about different energies available for us to tap into at any time, and then to share that understanding with others. As I wrote in chapter 1, one of my earliest experiences was with an ancient Egyptian, which I saw as a shadow on the wall. It turns out that wasn't actually my first experience with a Spirit Guide; when I was still a child, I had had a dream about a massive angel made of light, which I later came to understand was the energy of a guardian angel coming to watch over me. I believe this angel was giving me a window into a spiritual realm in a gentle way, one that wouldn't frighten me. Each entity came to me exactly as I needed them in the moment, bringing up the memories, emotions, and associations required for me to interpret their messages.

While my experiences are unique to me, the general theme is common: as we expand our openness to new ideas, our frame of reference grows. That gives Spirit more material to work with in their attempt to get through to us. The more our mind expands, the more we may find ourselves receiving guidance from eras, cultures, and schools of thought we may have been closed to in the past.

I recently had a powerful download during a meditation. As I sat quietly breathing in my bed, I was shown a vision of a person in maroon garments and told that I was standing in a place called the Kingdom of Nri, somewhere in present-day Nigeria. Then I was shown two large lions that came and sat next to me on my bed and heard a clear directive to go research a priest called Ezi, who would help me teach others more effectively. At the time, I had no idea why I was seeing this; I had never heard anything like this before. I had no frame of reference for the Kingdom of Nri or any being called Ezi.

When I came out of the meditation, of course I turned to good old Google and started to research. I learned that Ezi Nri was a title given to the religious and political leader of the Nri people, a group that lived in modern-day Nigeria through the Middle Ages. The Nri were a peaceful community that experienced rapid growth through the voluntary conversion of the people around them. They accepted everyone, including those who had been cast out or enslaved, and were uncommon in their region and time for being pacifists and abolitionists. I understood that I had received this vision to remind me to be peaceful, to free my mind, and to suggest that I can access the Kingdom of Nri when I'm reading for others to bring that energy to them. It also inspired me to look more into the history of different ancient cultures that have a strong connection to spirituality, like the Ezi Guide that came to me from the Kingdom of Nri, because doing so will be essential in developing as a teacher of this work. Like all spiritual lessons, something about this information felt oddly familiar, even though I couldn't make sense of it with my mind. It was as if my soul was remembering something it had always known to be true.

My experience with the Kingdom of Nri shows that Spirit Guides can come from anywhere—any cultural background, gender, ethnicity, time period, age, or religious affiliation. They can even be animals! Just a few months ago, I was meditating again on my bed when I was revisited by the same pair of lions, a male and a female. They came right up on the bed with me and cuddled together. Shortly thereafter, I saw a white wolf who led me through a mirror and into another realm—the animal realm, as I understood. I had been struggling with questions about the end-of-life decisions I had to make for my dog Phoenix (a process I will describe in greater detail in chapter 3). As I mulled over what to do, I instantly knew these animals were Guides for me in this period of my life.

I'd had a heads-up that something like this might happen. Just a few days before, my husband and I had been on a flight when his TV stopped working. The flight attendant came over to try to fix it, but there was just nothing to be done. My husband hadn't brought anything else to do, so I offered to switch seats with him and pulled out the book I was reading: ***Spirit Talker*** by Indigenous medium Shawn Leonard. I randomly flipped it open to the section on spirit animals. Reading Shawn's words, I understood the importance of connecting with spirit animals. This prepared me to encounter my own shortly thereafter.

Yes, Spirit Guides can break an in-flight entertainment system to get us to do our work—and they can wear any face, or even no face at all, while doing it. Just as we are not locked in our current incarnation, our Spirit Guides are far larger and greater than the form in which they appear to us. They only take such shapes to give us something more tangible for our mind to grab onto; they use symbolism to make their point. As you walk this path, you may find yourself connecting with Guides that are easy for you to understand, as well as others that take a little more figuring out. If you ever find yourself wavering, put out a clear intention: "I only wish to see the entities that are from the highest and best energy." This will assure you that what you are seeing is meant exactly for you.

Hearing Spirit's Voice

When we use our third eye or our dreams to visualize our Guides, we are employing the most common clair: ***clairvoyance***. It is also common to hear Guides through ***clairaudience*** or sense the messages they are giving with ***claircognizance***. Guides use different energies for us to discern who they are. Some have energy that feels very lighthearted, while others are more serious. They may also use different cadences, vocabulary, manners of speaking, and even accents to distinguish themselves from one another. Just like with their images, Guides' voices come in through our own frame of reference. The thoughts we hold about the way a Guide sounds are meant to trigger a whole set of meanings and associations within us, and those meanings and associations can help us discern the message the Guide is trying to convey.

As I explained in chapter 1, waiting to hear a specific voice other than my own was a big roadblock I had to overcome in my development as a psychic medium. I had to work to learn how to discern Spirit's voice from my inner monologue, because sometimes they seemed very similar. One thing that helped me in this endeavor was working on my claircognizance, so I could *feel* the difference in the vibration behind each voice. Even when Spirit's voice sounds a lot like me, it never *feels* like me. Each of my Spirit Guides has a definite and distinct energetic signature, a different wavelength governing their vibration that tips me off on how they can help.

Understanding this has helped me separate what's me from what's not me. This has been incredibly handy in the hormonal process I've been undergoing recently, as I encountered a voice that not only wasn't me, but also wasn't one of my Guides. Let me explain.

I'm fortunate to say that I've never really understood anxiety until I started doing this work. I experience a sort of high-pitched excitement sometimes when Spirit is trying to get through to me, but not the earthier, heavier sense of dread others have. While I've always had sympathy for people who experience strong anxiety, I've never really been able to empathize with it fully because it simply hasn't been something I've known on my own. Fear is something I do know well; it has a sort of dull, resigned quality to it, like two hands clapping together in a snowy landscape. Anxiety, I've learned, is more revved up, like the whine of a mosquito. I found this out because in the process of our move, and throughout many instances in the last two years, I started to hear little thoughts zing by like, *This isn't a good idea; it isn't safe. It's not going to work out. Your home is being ripped away from you!* And the even more dramatic, *Where are we going to live NOOOWWW?!* These thoughts would dive-bomb me like mosquitoes. *What was that?* my rational mind would think. And then a thought would whiz by again, causing me to stop what I was doing to try to hear it. This experience was coupled with a gasping, breathless feeling that comes with having been sucker punched in the gut.

When this happened, I'd do what I always do: run a simple cleansing ritual, then take a moment to feel myself connect down into the earth below and up to the heavens above, opening myself to receiving. And I'd quickly get a message: *Don't listen to that.* This message came from the familiar voice of my Guides, so I knew to trust it.

After this happened a few times, I started to wonder, what was this thing going "*neeeeeee!!!!*" by my ear? What was this sense of impending doom? I felt certain that it wasn't me, and my Guides were throwing their hands up claiming, ***It isn't us, either!*** I was clear about one thing, though: I didn't like it, and I didn't want its vibration around me at all.

Meanwhile, I'd been struggling with physical changes to my body that I knew were related to my hormones, so I asked my Guides to send me signs to indicate what could best support me during menopause. The answers came quickly. Within days I was seeing and hearing all sorts of things about anxiety, menopause, and medical interventions that can ease the hormonal process: an ad on TV, an interview on a podcast, a friend mentioning how much talking to her doctor had shifted things for her.

Yet I resisted. My mother's entire generation had gotten through menopause without medical treatment, and I really hoped that holistic methods like acupuncture could get me there, as they'd gotten me through so many things before. I felt wary, even a bit afraid, of asking for help from conventional medicine.

My Guides decided to make it even clearer for me. They sent me clients who would talk about anxiety, and as they did, I started to channel the feeling they were describing—that same nasty little mosquito cloud I'd finally experienced myself. "Oh, so *this* is anxiety," I communicated to my Guides, relieved to finally have a name for my issue. "I get it. Menopause is affecting more than just my physical body now. I guess I need help. Where should I find it?"

And if you're picturing them sending me to a shaman in the jungle or a yogi in a cave, think again, because they pointed me directly to my primary care provider. ***Just go see your doctor, MaryAnn,*** I heard. That's right—our Guides can give us instructions as clear and simple as that! The effect was immediate. The treatment my doctor prescribed worked like DEET, repelling any anxiety-mosquito that even thought to look my way. I was so relieved. I could finally approach the difficult feelings I had around moving from a balanced, grounded perspective—without the sense of doom. My physical symptoms subsided along with my mental ones, and I found a gentler landing for this new phase of life.

You may have noticed that the only borderline-woo part of this whole experience was the little bit of time I spent cleansing and grounding. There was no *om*-ing or ceremony involved; I barely even meditated about this issue, and I'm pretty sure I didn't burn a single candle. Instead, I just got curious and struck up a conversation with—yeah, I'm going to say it—the "voices in my head." And while some people may judge that, doing so allowed me to solve my own problem easily. Working with my Guides is a simple and painless way to address what challenges me, one that doesn't take me far out of my day-to-day life. It's authentically mine.

I will always encourage you to find your own authentic way to work with your Spirit Guides and your intuition in general. You don't have to do it like me—you can create rituals with incense and oils, write questions down and burn them (safely, though; ideally by a sink), practice automatic writing, or whatever works for you. Once you get really comfortable talking to your Guides, you may find as I have that formality is only really necessary when you're stuck in deep emotion and the fear is super-thick. Then you might want to pull some cards, *om* it out, do a guided meditation, etc. But the rest of the time, we can just . . . ask. It's really that simple.

When we ask, talking to our Spirit Guides the way we talk to our very best friends, we're naturally going to be authentic. Without the pomp, without even trying, we're going to end up our truest, most honest selves—no masks, no supposed-to-bes. That authenticity is the key to really hearing Spirit's voice. Being authentic takes a major load off our shoulders and also provides the best way for our Guides to get through to us. When we drop all pretense and just integrate our Guides into our lives, we set ourselves up to receive them whenever and however they wish to communicate with us. We indicate that we're willing to keep the door open for them to pipe up anytime.

That's when we start to receive downloads—when we're midway through the cracker aisle, reaching for our favorite snack, and receive a message about our family or the themes that are going to come up next in our lives or which beloved friend we need to text from the checkout line because they're having a difficult moment. We pause for an instant, receive what's given, and keep going about our day. In other words, when we relate with our Guides genuinely and openly, they reciprocate and do the same. We stop needing to reach up into the ether to communicate with them. Instead, we can just be here in this space and let them come in.

So who, specifically, do these voices belong to? How can we trust that we should listen to them?

The What vs. the Who

Most of us have questions about who our Guides are, how we knew them in the past, and where they reside now. And often our Guides themselves will answer them! I've had students connect with Guides by name or by face. Some Guides can inform us exactly where they came from or which dimension, planet, or aspect of heaven they are in now or when or how we knew them in a past life. I completely understand the drive to find out absolutely everything about a Guide and have indulged such urges myself!

Other times, though, where our Guides come from and who they might be are less clear. A Guide may not share these things with us, or we may not be able to interpret their message with a firm understanding. Sometimes this knowledge comes in time; other times it never arrives. In these cases, it's often simply not worth our time or energy to pursue it too deeply, because doing so can be a distraction from the more important work of interpreting and applying the Guide's message to our lives.

For instance, many channelers just pull in from a collective without having a clear sense of who or what they're channeling. Esther Hicks, as I mentioned a few pages back, has spent decades of her life channeling a collective voice called Abraham. I've never heard her worry about who Abraham is or how many beings they are or what they may look like; her only job is to deliver their message.

A few years ago, I began to work with a student, Dana, who does the same. She began to receive collective guidance for the general public and set up a YouTube channel to share the messages she receives. As I observe them, collective voices often seem to have the aim of reaching a wide audience; their teachings are often quite general. Dana doesn't do anything special to receive their guidance, because they have chosen her for this task and make it very simple for her to pass their message along. She just sits down with her spine straight, cleanses herself with holy water, lights a candle, closes her eyes, and breathes until they start to speak.

The first time I heard a collective voice, I was desperate to know who it was. I was a new mother and feeling insecure about being in such a feminine space, so I sat down into meditation and a feminine face came to me. "Who are you?" I asked, and then she changed her face to another feminine face, then another. I watched as she presented a slideshow of many people and things, flipping from one image to another—people from all walks of life, animal faces, scenes of nature, all of it. ***I have been all things and I am all things,*** I heard. I realized it didn't matter what I called her because she could use any name or any face. Those earthly depictions were just for my benefit so that I could understand her. Her essence went far beyond any single identity.

Today, I'm much more comfortable receiving guidance from beings I can't quite identify—quite frequently, actually! In many cases, identifying them would simply take time that I don't have. If I'm being told to turn left or right, I don't argue. I've already put out the prayer that I will only be contacted by beings who work in service of the highest and greatest good—I don't need to know more about them. I notice a lot of people get hung up on this point, so I want to be really clear about it: it's not the *who* that makes the message powerful or significant, it's the *what.* In other words, it doesn't matter how the message comes; it only matters what that message is and how you're going to apply it to your life.

Think about it this way. If you're going to work with a healer or a therapist, you want to know they are qualified to do their work. That's important. But it's their methodology and their talent that is most helpful to you, not their personality. That's why with Guides, if they don't readily indicate who they are, I encourage you to release your need to know and just focus on what they tell you. Ask, "What is it you need me to know?" They will show you through visions in your third eye or send you a dream, and if you can't fully understand, you can always get out some cards, a pendulum, or another tool to help you receive the message.

When we focus on the what instead of the who, we realize that the whole question of who our Guides are can simply be a distraction from the greater work at hand. It's a rabbit hole that doesn't serve us nearly as much as the messages our Guides have to offer. So while it's completely natural to want answers to these questions, I find it's better to accept the answers when they come without putting too much energy into searching for more information. We're far better served by investing in sharpening our interpretation of the messages we receive and putting them into action in our everyday life.

No matter how many Guides we channel or where they come from, our Guides will always agree on what's best for us. They may "yes-and" each other, offering new ideas and perspectives, but their philosophies never clash with or contradict one another. In fact, hearing contradictory advice is a clear sign that it's time to consider whether you're getting in your own way. This is yet another reason we don't necessarily need to know who our Guides are or where their guidance is coming from; frequently, when we do, we start to put too much energy and opinion into our interpretation, thinking that a Guide from this place or time will have this opinion and a Guide from that place or time will have another. Our Guides often have good reason for showing or not showing us who they are. It's up to us to trust that.

In rare circumstances, a Guide may ask us to go to work to figure out who they are. This is when it can be helpful to look toward Guides others have met and channeled in the past, to expand our frame of reference so we can process more information. In these cases, I suggest taking a look at the decks put out by the wonderful Kyle Gray, who has a true talent for naming and identifying different Guides. Using one of his decks along with your own intuition can help you discern who you may be talking to at any given time.

Sometimes Guides will jump out of other lightworkers' materials to show you who they are. I was working with Kyle's ***Keepers of the Light Oracle Cards*** deck one day when I gasped. Somehow, I had stumbled upon an image I hadn't seen before—or, to be more precise, I hadn't seen the *card* before, though the image it held was completely familiar to me. I found myself looking into the eyes of a Guide I'd seen many times with my third eye. Underneath this familiar Guide was a name I hadn't heard before, and that I frankly struggle to remember to this day: Melchizedek. I've just always called this Guide "Joe." "Melchizedek" is a mouthful, and I guess it's just far enough outside my frame of reference that I can't keep track of it. But Joe? Sure, I know Joe, he's my guy! And in the end, Joe's role in my life, the things he comes to show me and guide me through, are far more important than what I call him . . . so Joe it is!

Regardless of who they are, all our Guides will feel instantly familiar to us. We'll have the sense we're talking to someone who knows us really, really well, like a long-lost friend or a loving caregiver from our childhood who exists just beyond what our memory can grasp. Understanding this can help us hear their voice more clearly and make the most sense of the message they have to give.

In the next exercise, you'll have a chance to see the Guides in your sphere who are ready to show themselves to you.

EXERCISE: SPEED-MEETING YOUR GUIDES

Take the time to read through this guided visualization at least twice before beginning, so you can go through the steps without opening your eyes. As you do so, don't worry too much about getting all the steps just right; do your best, but let your intuition lead you. Far too many of my students worry that they're meditating wrong! I think that's a ridiculous concept because there is no such thing as right or wrong when it comes to meditation, as long as your intention is for and from the greatest and highest good; just keep at it and see what arises. Trust that you will intuitively gravitate toward the parts of the meditation that are most authentic to you.

First, cleanse yourself with something like sage, incense, or palo santo (in a pinch, just imagine yourself doing it!). Then feel your energy grounding down into the earth, and connect your crown to the spiritual energies above. Set a timer for five minutes to begin.

Imagine yourself sitting at a table with an empty chair across from you. You can sit in a simple room, in a field of grass, or anywhere you'd like! Now, as you take a deep breath, we're going to invite several Guides to sit across from you one by one. Ask for the first one to appear.

Allow their form to take shape. You may recognize this Guide from the Meet Your Guide exercise or from a vision or dream you've had in the past. They may also be brand-new to you! Take a moment to notice all you can about this Guide—the colors on and around them, the clothes they wear, their features, how you feel. If there is any sound, vibration, smell, or taste associated with them, make a mental note of it, as this may be a way for you to know when you are communicating with this Guide in the future.

Once you've studied the Guide, you can start to ask them questions. You can ask anything you want! You may start with who they are or where they are from, but you may also choose to focus on what area of your life they are here to help with, or even what they'd like to say to you in the moment. Try not to put too much emphasis on asking them for help right now; the greater goal is to understand what kind of help they can give so you can more easily call upon them in the future. Keep breathing deeply, letting your body relax in the meditation.

When you feel complete with this Guide, let them fade away. Keep breathing until the next one takes shape. It may be a minute or two between Guides; practice patience as you wait. Then follow the same process for the next Guide. Allow yourself to meet at least three Guides this way before concluding.

I highly recommend that you take a few minutes to write down what you learned before concluding the session.

Chapter 3

DESTINATION UNKNOWN

GETTING TO KNOW YOUR GUIDES IS ONE THING. LIVING IN CONnection with them is something else entirely. In this world, society teaches us that we should know where we're going: we should aim for this degree or this achievement or this career and pursue it, come what may. We should make a plan, then stick to it. Otherwise, what are we doing, careening through life without a tether? That's an irresponsible way to live, our culture says, and we should avoid it at all costs by picking out one point on the map, deciding on a route to take us there, and driving that route.

Living in connection with our Guides forces us to shift our thinking. Our Guides may pick a point on the map and say, ***Head in that direction!*** But then, midway through the journey, they may throw out a random, ***Hang a left!*** "Hold on," we'll reply, "that'll loop us back to where we started!" ***Left!*** they'll repeat. And what do we do in that situation? We hang that left, even though it makes zero sense, because that's what our Guides told us to do.

Contrary to what our world may have us believe, what I just described isn't careening through life without a tether. Instead, it's a process of releasing what we think we should be tethered to, and tethering ourselves to our Guides instead. This doesn't mean we can't set goals or work toward greater things. We can still do that—but we must trust that when our Guides seemingly take us off course, it's for a reason, because there's some beautiful vista or roadside attraction we need to see before we get to our destination. We believe in our very core that our Guides have our best interest at heart and that there are no detours . . . not really. Everything we are guided to do is in service of our soul's greater evolution.

In truth, we don't have to consciously know where we're going, because our Guides can point us to our deepest inner knowing. This core part of us understands where we've been, why we are where we are now, and where we're headed—in this life and in others.

Letting go is easier said than done, though, right? It's natural for us to have expectations about where our lives are going or what they're supposed to look like. These expectations keep us feeling safe. But they do so at a cost: they keep our lives small, existing right inside the scope of what we can imagine is possible. I want more for you. I suspect you do, too, which is why you're reading this book. We're far better served by an unimaginably big life, one that takes twists and turns more wonderful than we could ever dream up and that surprises us with greater and more fantastic things around every corner. This is what happens when we rely on and trust that part of our soul that is co-creating right alongside Spirit. This is the part of us that is in contact with our Spirit Guides, who are here to show us the way.

It can be scary to not know what's going to happen, to have to sit and wait, relying on divine timing. It can be frustrating to feel like we are making progress in one direction only to be told to turn around and walk the opposite way. Yet trust can and will overcome that frustration, and the more we ask our Guides to show us signs to affirm our faith, the easier it becomes to access this trust. This is a great time to change our perspective, shifting how we view fear and realizing that we ourselves are a part of our own story, with the power to co-create alongside our Guides. We recognize that while we are surrendering to their wisdom, that is quite an empowered position in which to be because it opens worlds to us that we previously thought could only exist in a dream.

The very first step to this wild and unpredictable process is releasing the urge to control the outcome.

Releasing the Outcome

That's right—like a road trip without a defined end point, we're best served when we let go of our ideas of where we think we're going and open ourselves to where the road of life takes us.

Surrendering the plans our minds have made to what our highest being intends for us is not an easy task. It doesn't happen in a single instant, either; rather, it's a series of small realizations followed by miniature releases, as we shift our focus from our desired outcome to the journey it takes to get there and everything we have to learn along the way.

Releasing our perceived control of the outcome is a tricky topic in spiritual circles, especially because many of us are focused on manifesting what we want. And manifesting is certainly important work! Yet as even the best manifesting teachers will tell us, we do ourselves a great disservice when we repeat the lie that we are absolutely certain what is best for us. We don't have to know what the future is going to look like; what we're best at is knowing what it should *feel* like. Often the very best thing is outside our frame of reference, and our mind needs to expand before we can conceive it. Focusing our manifestation on the way we want to feel, on the longing within us that will be fulfilled by the object or situation that we desire, is most important. We have to trust that the Universe is going to show us what we need to do to reach that feeling. This doesn't mean don't manifest—we can still make our lists, our vision boards, all of it. And we can still speak our future into existence, talking about things as if they're already happening. But our Guides don't want us to just skip to the good part, which is the end result. We have to be curious and excited about *how* our Guides get us there as well. This is the part where the real work happens—the dance between you and Spirit that is behind everything I teach.

While I absolutely encourage you to trust yourself and your knowing, I also encourage you to be open to that which lies beyond it—because this is the area in which miracles can take place. It helps to know what you want and to go for it, but don't be surprised if you realize along the way that something else is going to work better for you. Trust that your Guides will show you the best outcome. It may not look exactly like what you thought you were manifesting, but it will hold the same energy.

When my husband and I first started to discuss putting our house on the market—or rather, when he first suggested it to a highly resistant me—one of the biggest thoughts in my head was that I didn't know where we were going to end up. And if I didn't know where we were going to end up, fear told me we were probably going to end up without having any home to go to at all (even though this was highly unlikely). I've been a homeowner since my twenties. Going back to renting, even temporarily while our new home was being built, felt like a step backward. Plus, I didn't know how I would be able to invest my energy in a rental. I wanted a home that felt like mine, and in my mind a rental could never feel that way.

My Guides assured me that things would work out better than I imagined and that, like so many things that bring up resistance, there would be unexpected positives to renting a home. So when our home on Long Island sold, I put on my brightest face and called a rental agent.

We toured several places that didn't feel right, even though they had a lot going for them on paper. They ticked all the boxes I'd assured our rental agent needed to be ticked. Not knowing what to do, she decided to show us some places that ***didn't*** tick all the boxes and see how we responded.

She took us out to a three-bedroom ranch home in a sweet town not far from our old house. The major upside to this home was that the owners were willing to rent it year-round, instead of holding out for the high summer prices New Yorkers are willing to pay. When I saw the house on the outside, I didn't think much of it, though I noted it was the same color and had a similar house number as the one we'd just sold. But I'd asked for a sign, and a cardinal—which are signs for me—was sitting on a bike in the open garage. Then we walked inside and I felt the house's energy, and something came alive in me.

I walked through the house feeling stronger and stronger energies of the people who had lived there before us. They had been there a long time, I could sense, and had really loved the space. Everything felt comfortable, normal, lived-in. While my husband and the agent were talking in the kitchen, I felt myself called to go down to the basement. It's an old-school, partially finished basement, with low light, furniture that is clean and functional but much older than that in the upstairs of the house, pictures of trains and owls, and tons of military memorabilia. It gave me grandfather feels in all the good ways. I could sense that an older gentleman had spent a lot of time down there, collecting, tinkering, and putting his love into the space. "Hi, Grandpa," I whispered, and the energy of the room received my greeting. ***I'm so glad you're here,*** I heard in response. ***I'm so glad you picked us, because we picked you.***

When I came back upstairs, Grandpa's energy came up with me. Suddenly I saw the house in a whole new light. While it had felt loved and lived in before, I now felt that ***I*** loved it and that ***I*** lived in it. I said to my husband,

"I don't need to look any further." He, being less fussy than I about these things, looked relieved. "We'll take it," he told the rental agent.

There was (and still is) a special energy in the house because I see it through Grandpa's eyes. Once we moved in, I came to realize this was a regular occurrence. Grandpa just stops in sometimes to make sure we're taking good care of the place and loving it as he would.

After we'd been there about a month, my daughter came to visit. She arrived while my husband and I were out, so we hid a key for her, giving her an hour or two in the house on her own. When we arrived, I asked, "How do you like the house?"

"Oh, it's really cute," she answered, smiling. "Who's the guy in the basement?"

A few weeks after that my son came to stay. He, too, had a vision of an older gentleman downstairs, and it was as positive an experience for him as it was for the rest of us.

Had I gone off my checklist alone, I never would have picked this house. But in the end, it gave me all the feelings I wanted from a home: a sense of connection and ownership, channeled through Grandpa.

Manifesting is often blocked by fear. Fear tells us we need to have exactly this or exactly that to be OK, while our higher selves are manifesting what things feel like, not what they look like. It therefore often takes a strong feeling to break through the image fear has sold us so our real dream can come true.

One of my students, Shayla, spent most of her career in the health industry, working behind the scenes with big pharma. Though she was trained as a registered nurse, she had never worked directly with patients, and she found herself getting increasingly frustrated by a job that she felt didn't give her a sense of purpose. Yet financially she was doing very well, and she received huge accolades from her colleagues and superiors. She was trapped in a golden cage.

Shayla initially wanted to break out of that cage and transition into a more traditional nursing career. "I'm ready to leave this soul-sucking career behind!" she announced triumphantly. But though she longed to become a nurse in the traditional sense, she found herself frozen at the precipice of change. She had a kid in college and a car payment, both of which would be squeezed by the shift in income, and though her home wasn't far from the nearest hospital, the traffic in her city would increase her daily commute by more than an hour. As she started to work with Spirit, she realized she could keep her day job while beginning the healing work her soul was calling her to do. She went to massage school and took a training program to become a death doula. Then she hung out her shingle as a spiritual and therapeutic companion for people at the end of life.

In the first few years of her new practice, Shayla didn't make much money. It was convenient for her to keep receiving her corporate salary while she waited for her youngest to graduate and paid off her car. By the time she really got the hang of her new career, her income and expenses had balanced more. She eventually did quit her big pharma career. Everything aligned in the perfect time and much better than she could have ever imagined when she dreamed of using her nursing degree.

Shayla didn't misstep by getting a nursing degree she never really used. Each pit stop on the road toward her goal was essential, however meandering that road may have been. By focusing on how she wanted to feel and releasing control of the outcome, she allowed Spirit to take the lead and found a greater resolution than she could have manifested through her imagination alone.

Releasing the outcome is never easy. It isn't something we learn to do once and for all, either. Most of us will spend a lot of our life struggling to release the outcome, no matter how many times we learn the lesson. And there are some outcomes that are just too tragic to ever really accept. We may never know exactly why our Guides lead us through such challenges. All we can do is keep breathing and keep trying to find faith.

Over the last few years, I have worked with a client, Beth, whose husband Len received a devastating cancer diagnosis in his late forties. While he followed his doctor's orders, immediately going through the process of chemotherapy and radiation, she got to work reorganizing their lives so he could still find joy in his days. She made sure she and Len had plenty of quality time together with their kids, all the while praying, manifesting, and doing everything she could on the spiritual level to bring him to healing. The first time we spoke after his diagnosis, she seemed sure he would recover.

She held on to that conviction even when the results of his treatment were not as good as expected. She continued to hold on as he began to weaken, worried that if she let go, she would accidentally manifest his death.

I found this thinking concerning—not Beth's faith or hope, but her overblown sense of responsibility in the matter. In my field, I hear plenty of stories of miracles. I know these miracles are possible, but they are only possible when they align with the greater plan. Releasing the outcome means that while we still hope for the best and work to bring it about, we also accept when what is right on one level is also incredibly, painfully, devastatingly wrong on every single other level imaginable. These are the moments when the only thing we can do is summon our free will in order to keep believing. We have to trust that what's happened is part of our soul's story; and at the same time, we have to grieve the fact that the only world we've known in this lifetime has been blown apart, that things are terribly unfair, and that we will never be the same.

This is what Beth was faced with as, just a year after Len's diagnosis, it became clear that there was nothing he, she, the doctors, or all the Guides in the world could do, because this disease would inevitably be the end of his life. Eventually she came back to me with the worst news of all: her beloved Len had passed away.

Tragedy challenges the faith of nearly everyone who experiences it. If we think we're in control of everything around us or that good fortune is a reward for good behavior, we suffer even more. The truth is impossible things sometimes happen to people and they have nothing to do with how hard they prayed or what they put on their vision board, because some things are simply out of our control. These are the times when we really need to lean on our Guides, angels, and loved ones, the times we need to connect with our own idea of God and the Universe and work to decipher what we are meant to learn from the experience, even as we mourn deeply for the way we wish things had gone.

Doing so requires free will. It requires us to go above what's easy and continue to *try* to trust the Universe, even if we repeatedly fail. This is the true gift we have been given in this human incarnation: the opportunity to choose, even the slightest bit, how we respond to the events around us.

The Role of Free Will

Free will governs how we respond to the world around us. It helps determine how we will interpret the events in our lives that point toward our lessons, as well as the choices we will make based on those interpretations. Using our free will to look for the positive is one of the best ways we can co-create with Spirit. It helps our Guides show us our lessons when things are uncomfortable.

I've tried to remember this as I walk through menopause. Like so many women before me, I'm super-challenged by the changes in my body. My hair isn't as thick as it used to be; it's harder to maintain my weight; my temperature is all over the place; and I'm moodier than I've ever been. But my Guides keep asking me to look for the positives, so I'm working to listen to their wisdom and put my energy there as much as I can.

I'm smack-dab in the middle of this work, so here's what I've got so far. First of all, I don't get my period anymore, which is pretty great. That means I don't need to lug around all these supplies and worry that I might get any unpleasant surprises. I also have this great opportunity to examine my vanity and embrace the imperfections of a human body. For the first time ever, I took a six-month break from pushing myself at the gym because I was just so tired, and it was so lovely to accept that my body needs rest. And I've gained *so much* wisdom. Wisdom is by far the greatest gift I've gotten from menopause. I feel that it's even easier to discern what is right and wrong for me and I have more to offer the world on a spiritual level.

So far, using my free will is paying off. Everything changed once I started to shift my perspective and celebrate menopause. I started to feel much better. I began giving back the same validation I have been so grateful to receive from other women who have gone through the process, assuring others, "No, you aren't crazy: you're just hormonal!" I've tried new healing techniques and been much kinder on my body—eating better, drinking more water and less wine, and finding new ways to relax.

That's how we jump from one timeline to another. We can be going down a particular path, with particular life circumstances coming our way to teach us our lessons, and we can use our free will to just hop over to something else. It doesn't always change the external circumstances right now, but it may affect what's coming down the line.

The concept of timelines is a bit tricky, so let me explain. We can take many paths in life. We are constantly faced with choices that could change which timeline we are on. This is what our free will is for: it's what allows us to choose. As a psychic, I can tap into one or maybe two timelines, because I do know what the Universe has in store for you but I don't know what you're going to choose. And based on what you choose, the Universe may present you with something entirely different.

As co-creators of the Universe, we are generating our own story by living it. We came in with these things to learn and what will be will be—there is some degree of mystery there—but we can always control how we react to what has taken place, which affects things going forward. When we shift our perspective, we hop onto a timeline that can bring even more good things our way.

But don't worry—even when we miss an opportunity to use our free will, our Guides will show up with new ones.

My student Johnny was on the smaller side when he was growing up. He described his younger self as skinny and "more into the library than the football field," which was hard as a boy in a small town, where photos of teenage athletes regularly graced the front page of the local newspaper. His parents had taught him to be nonviolent to a fault, and he didn't have great social skills by nature. All of this came to a head in middle school, when he started being bullied. He was an easy target, turning inward instead of fighting back. As an adult, this morphed into a pattern of anxiety and depression. Stress itself became a bully for Johnny; he simply couldn't manage the pressures of work and adult life without turning inward yet again and feeling beaten up by it all.

When he first started coming to my workshops to develop his intuitive self, I felt this energy from him and read him in the group. His Guides showed me how he'd been bullied and mocked, and Johnny affirmed the pattern was still alive and well. A colleague had started to give him extra work on the side, and his manager was just allowing it to happen. Hearing this, the others in the group were immediately compassionate, and I could see that he was basking in their love. Yet this, too, concerned me; it seemed like Johnny put too much stock in what other people thought of him and didn't have a strong image of who he was beyond that.

As Johnny started working with his Guides, he started coming across online content about boundaries. He signed up for a program to help people set boundaries and was surprised to find that the first few modules were about compassion, self-love, and self-care. Johnny had no idea his self-esteem was so low, but the course helped him immensely. His Guides increasingly led him to opportunities to utilize his free will and set boundaries with his shiny new spine: first with his colleague and manager at work, then in a new romantic relationship that he chose to walk away from after some red flags cropped up way too soon. In the years we worked together, things started to get much better for Johnny, and even when things didn't go his way, he was able to face them with more strength and resilience. By activating his free will, Johnny switched timelines and was able to manifest something new.

While it doesn't give us *control,* our free will does give us *influence,* and it helps us choose which direction our lives will take going forward. This doesn't always mean we can alter outward events, but it does mean we can affect how we respond to them, opening ourselves to the highest and best good that is waiting for us. Accepting that is key, because once we do, we realize our lives are the material for the lessons we have to learn—not by accident, but by intention—and the challenges that arise have been selected just for us, allowing for even greater spiritual evolution.

Follow What Presents Itself

As we travel through the world listening to guidance and using our free will, we are called to face life exactly as it is. We can read our daily experiences like a set of Tarot cards, observing what presents itself and finding meaning within it. The symbols, synchronicities, and experiences of our life show us what we're here to learn.

I haven't yet told you about one of the major factors that affected our decision to sell our home. Our beloved golden retriever Phoenix was getting older and had developed dementia. He'd lived his whole life in our home with us, helping us raise the kids through their teenage years as a blended family. I couldn't imagine taking him away from it, and especially from the grassy field behind our plot where he loved to run. Our boys called it the "Field of

Dreams" after the Kevin Costner movie, because they liked to play baseball there, and the name stuck. As Phoenix aged and his health declined, I'd take him out to the Field of Dreams and he'd always perk up, mustering a little energy to trot around even when he couldn't chase and catch the way he used to.

I cited Phoenix as a major reason not to move when the idea was first presented to me. I knew I couldn't prolong his life, but I wanted to make it as easy and comfortable for him as I could at the end. But as time went on, I began to hear quite clearly that it wouldn't be an issue; that his life would naturally come to a close before we moved to our rental. All around me, people were hinting that it might be time to put Phoenix to sleep. And perhaps it would have been a good time—but I didn't feel he was ready yet. "Please show me," I asked my Guides. "Let me know when it's time, and I'll listen, I promise."

One day after a hard visit to the vet I was fretting over the issue. On the one hand, I worried that I wouldn't know when it was time and Phoenix would suffer unnecessarily, and on the other hand, I worried that I'd end his life sooner than he wanted. It may feel out of character, but I absolutely struggle with doubts like this, especially around such a difficult decision as putting my beloved dog to sleep. As I looked at Phoenix dozing peacefully on the floor, I went from questioning to badgering Spirit, prodding my Guides for more and more detail while still trying to avoid yes or no questions like I always do. I knew I needed to calm down and center my energy, but I felt too distressed to figure out how to do so. Then I heard, ***Pull a card.*** Thank you, Guides! I instantly knew that a card would give me the clarity I needed and allow me to let the issue be, so I reached for Colette Baron-Reid's ***Enchanted Map Oracle Cards*** deck.

The card I pulled depicted three fairies sitting contentedly on a collection of multicolored eggs surrounded by butterflies. Stretched out all around them is a large field of grass and wildflowers. The card is called "Field of Dreams."

I sat holding it with tears in my eyes. *OK, I'll know when,* I thought to myself. The confirmation reminded me who I was and that my Guides are always there to lead me toward the highest and best. This conviction allowed me to relax my need to control and use my free will to trust that when the moment was there, I'd know.

Seeing the Field of Dreams card affirmed that my Guides are always on my side, and this allowed me to release my need to control even as I faced the enormous grief of losing Phoenix. Then one morning I woke up hearing wind chimes and, somehow, I just knew. The chimes were there to tell me. I went to my family and together we made the heart-wrenching decision to let our sweet old dog go.

Grief doesn't just break our hearts; it breaks them open. In the middle of this challenging experience of moving, I got the opportunity to remember what really makes a home and a family: connection, love, being together. I feel that my life circumstances showed me exactly what I needed to see and called me to feel exactly what I needed to feel to face my challenge. Phoenix's death was a part of that somehow.

Receiving the Field of Dreams card was also an undeniable synchronicity. Synchronicities come through in our lives in ways that are authentic to us and only us. They show us the messages meant for us.

One of my students had the call to become a healer but didn't know how. Carol was looking into reiki, energy healing, and more formal methods like chiropractics, but didn't have any idea what to choose. She asked me for advice on this, but all I heard was, *Tell her to ask for a sign.* With that I know my Guides want the other person to connect with their own Guides; it's a sort of weaning off that Magic 8 Ball dependency I mentioned in the introduction of this book. So Carol asked for a sign, and a few days later she went on Instagram and saw an advertisement for a somatic healing seminar. *OK,* she thought, *but doesn't that just mean my phone is listening to me or using cookies to guess what kind of advertisements I'd like to see? Fine,* her Guides replied, *we'll try again later.* Within days she had overheard others talking about somatic healing three more times—once at a coffee shop, again in the grocery store checkout line, and a third time at a summer barbecue. Carol finally got it. She signed up for the seminar she'd seen advertised online.

Think of it this way: if we're playing a game with our Guides, our own lives are the court on which the game is played. Our lives demonstrate to us what our Guides are trying to verbalize. They do it in a way that is authentic to us—not to this person or that other person, but to *us*, specifically.

Another student of this work, Mathilde, learned this when she and her husband pursued their dream of purchasing an off-grid property in the

French countryside near where she'd grown up. They wanted to find a piece of land tucked away from the world where they could grow old together, so they waited for a market high, sold their house in the city, and relocated to a rental in Provence. They looked for three years, but nothing suitable was within their budget—not only that, but between an increase in land prices and inflation, it felt like the longer they looked, the further out of budget their dreams became. Their health started to suffer as they experienced the stress of being ungrounded and longing for home. Mathilde explained, "We were doing vision boards, Post-it notes, guided meditations, all of that. And I knew that stuff works—I'd read *The Secret* in my twenties when I was dead broke and manifested $100,000 within the year—but it wasn't working. Actually, it was making us sick."

Mathilde asked for higher guidance to help her understand what this all meant in her life. She saw that she was holding strongly to an image of success. "I wanted an off-grid house in France—that part was real," she explained. "But did it really have to be an Instagrammable dream house I could live in forever? When I looked at it more closely, I realized that was just what my ego wanted. And I was at a point in my life where I just didn't want to listen to my ego anymore." Mathilde looked back and realized that she had seen house after house that could have met a lot of her needs, and she was just ignoring them all because her ego couldn't accept what Spirit was offering her.

Mathilde and her husband decided to lower their expectations and see if they could find a place that felt right, even if it didn't meet all their baseline requirements. Shortly after that a property came up for sale that only fit about 60% of their manifestation list. Something called to them anyway.

Mathilde and her husband decided to pull cards to help them understand why their Guides were leading them to something that fell so short of their dreams. Using the *OSHO Zen Tarot* deck, they got the Moment to Moment card, which depicts a monk crossing a rainbow river on a series of stepping stones. Mathilde interpreted the card to mean the house was a stepping stone that would help them get the dream they wanted. "I saw how I was being unrealistic," she said. "I wanted much more than what was available at the time. I'd had that pattern for a long time: fighting the Universe, wanting things to be absolutely perfect, refusing to accept what is. I wanted to be special, and a special person always gets her dream house for a screaming bargain, right?! Once I saw the house as a stepping stone, I felt *so much relief*. We don't actually need that much right now, and can switch again when we're older." Her Guides had used the opportunity to push her to do the bigger work around ego, self-worth, and expectations and offered her a workable solution in the end.

Mathilde and her husband gained huge spiritual lessons from the process, learning about compromise, patience (more on that in chapter 6!), and accepting what is. They also got a chance to get clear about what was really important to them. Through presenting them with limited options, Spirit showed them how to do this in a way they couldn't have imagined before.

I can't tell you how many times I've heard students say some version of, "I was doing so well before. I was charging my crystals in the moonlight, using my cards, all of it. And now I haven't had time for any of that, so I don't know which way to turn next." Sometimes these people are just so busy—they're running businesses and homes and families. They're just trying to get their eight hours of sleep and their twice-weekly workouts and some healthy eating in somehow, and spirituality feels like this extra thing tacked onto the rest. While I do advocate some sort of spiritual practice whenever possible, sometimes life just doesn't allow for it. I try to explain this, but we are so incredibly hard on ourselves that we often don't believe we can let up a little and still be spiritual.

The truth is that our Guides are often the ones supporting us with the tools we need in our busy lives. They're the ones that brought us that podcast about sleep hygiene, that new teacher at the gym, that dietary advice we're trying to follow. It's our spiritual imperative to follow where they lead us, and—if you can believe me—*following is spiritual enough*. Sure, it's good to get in a twenty-minute meditation when we can, but even two minutes will do. It's enough to grab that two minutes in the car when you're early to pick up the kids or while you're waiting for the pasta water to boil. It's even enough to just take a breath while you feel the shower water run over your head, down your body, and to your toes. If life is leading you to very full days, it's also leading you to find the spirituality within them wherever and however you can.

Other times, our Guides will call us to create a spiritual practice with a firm schedule. Jess, a student of mine who is CEO of a big and busy business, has found great success by scheduling a morning routine. She reserves ninety minutes every morning for meditation and other practices because she simply can't fit them into her day otherwise. This isn't the right setup for every busy person, but Jess finds it's what her life requires, so she follows it.

Each of us has an individual journey, and every one of them takes many twists and turns. We will walk left only to run back to the right; we will sometimes take a direct route from point A to point B, and other times we will find ourselves meandering so much it's hard to believe we're actually getting anywhere. Our Guides want us to trust that we are always on the path, always getting somewhere, and we're doing everything exactly right. When we release control of the outcome, activate our free will to make confident decisions, and follow what our life gives us, we find that we can face the unknown without fear. This surrendering to the unknown is a graduation of sorts. It's the moment when we move from playing with spirituality to truly living a spiritual life.

EXERCISE: DIVINE MIRROR

For this exercise, you'll need a mirror. Low lighting or candlelight may help set the mood, but make sure you can still see yourself clearly.

Take a moment to cleanse the space and then ground yourself, feeling your roots reaching down and connecting to the earth while your crown reaches up to let the light in.

Enter a short meditation to ask your Guides to show you who you really are. Remember, this is their biggest and most important work: to show us our authentic selves. That includes our very human flaws, yes, but also the truth of the divine beings we are. Close your eyes and set your intention, asking to see that truth, and breathe there for a minute or two.

When you're ready, open your eyes and look into the mirror. Really study your own face—your eyes, your cheeks, the expression of your mouth. If you have fine lines or marks on your face, appreciate them: see them as part of this beautiful piece of art the creator has put on earth. Keep studying and breathing. Blink as needed, but don't look away.

After a few minutes, you may notice the lines begin to blur or the colors start to shift. Continue to look steadily into the mirror. Over time, your own divinity will reveal itself to you. This is the true you. This is the one who can face whatever comes. This is the one who is ready for the unknown.

When you feel complete with this exercise, offer gratitude to yourself, your highest knowing, your Guides, and Spirit—which, like you and the divine self you just saw in the mirror, are in fact one and the same. Close the practice and step back into the world, knowing that you are a divine being.

Chapter 4
BACKSEAT DRIVER

AS WE LEARN TO CONNECT MORE DEEPLY WITH OUR SPIRIT Guides, it's also important to explore what it means to connect with our loved ones on the Other Side.

So many of us are invested in our loved ones being a part of our team. It's natural to want the people we know and miss to be there guiding us, especially early in our psychic development. We know our loved ones so well; we easily recognize them, readily believe them, and are comfortable conversing with them casually, just as we did when they were alive. Their very presence is comforting to us. So wouldn't it be nice if our entire team were made up of those we once spent time with on this physical plane?

Compared to connecting to loved ones, working with our Spirit Guides can be a little less comfortable. While they'll always *feel* familiar, we can struggle to wrap our minds around who they are, what they sound like, and why they've come to us specifically. Many who travel this path really seek to comprehend these sorts of details, and with Spirit Guides, they aren't always clear. We may get an answer we don't understand, such as that a Spirit Guide comes from another time or space, is another species of being, is a collective, or is from a religion we aren't connected to in this lifetime—everything we discussed in chapter 2. We may also get no answer at all, or just the basics without the details. It takes work to quiet the mind and just listen to what our Guides have to say.

Beyond that, we often really miss our loved ones. Some of us are struggling with grief at their passing. Others have gone through the acute stage of grief and simply long to make connection. This longing, while an important part of our spiritual process, can make it harder for them to get through to us.

Lucky for us, our loved ones *are* on our team, and connecting with them can help us develop a relationship with the rest of its members. While they aren't Spirit Guides in the formal sense, our loved ones who have passed play such an important role in guiding our way in this life that the rest of this chapter will be all about them.

The Role of Loved Ones

That's right—loved ones are not Spirit Guides, but they are an invaluable part of our team. When it comes to guiding us along our journey, loved ones play an important role.

In chapter 1 I wrote about my friend Anne Marie who told me to *Eat all the Thanksgiving dinner, and then some.* With this message, Anne Marie was indicating that in the process of passing on from this plane, one of the things her soul had learned was that her habit of stressing about staying fit had cost her some joy in life. Anne Marie came through to give me this message because she knew that I have that same habit and it is harmful for me just as it was for her. But in sharing this she didn't actually tell me anything new; I'm aware that vanity doesn't serve me much of the time, and that awareness runs through my mind often, manifesting as a desire to let go and just enjoy life as it is. She was simply weighing in on my own inner guidance. This is exactly what our loved ones on the Other Side do: they tap into what our Guides are already telling us and affirm for us that it is, in fact, our highest truth.

Loved ones are all about affirmation. They remind us that we are loved, accompanied, and supported on our journey. We frequently talk to them or think of them when we go through something that reminds us of the role they played in our life, and they're listening. When I channel loved ones for others, they often mention the thoughts they pick up on and affirm which ones are true.

Loved ones are all about affirmation.

For instance, I was recently working with my student Leigh, who is a new mother. Her infant daughter, while otherwise healthy, is not putting on weight the way her pediatrician hopes to see. In one of our conversations I was interrupted by Leigh's father, who was himself a pediatrician in life. He started giving advice about how she should feed the baby, but his ideas weren't unfamiliar to her; as Leigh confirmed, he was selecting from the options her pediatrician had offered. "When I was in the doctor's office and hearing these options, I wished I could just run them by my dad," Leigh explained. "I was pretty sure I knew what I needed to do, but I just needed the confirmation." Her father had heard her wish and had come through me to provide it. He went on to assure Leigh that she was doing a great job as a mother and that though he had passed on, he was still there, observing and delighting in her son. He offered his protection and his love in a vulnerable time.

In a more general sense, loved ones are here to teach us what life is about: forgiveness, love, and what's really important. It's their role to love us through painful things that feel like they don't serve us and, when things hurt anyway, to help us accept the lessons within that pain. They reassure us that we are not alone, and by doing so, they remind us that death is not the end; that when we ourselves die, some part of our story will live on to help those we leave behind.

On most topics, therefore, loved ones don't really provide much direct guidance. But every rule has its exceptions: for instance, like Anne Marie, they may share wisdom that reflects something you went through together in life, which they came to understand better as they transitioned out, in a process called *life review*. Life review is the sort of school we undertake when we die that shows us, in a greater sense, what we came here to learn—the assignments we understood, the assignments we worked toward but didn't complete, and the assignments we missed completely. Loved ones may also weigh in on questions we have asked them (or, like Leigh, wished we could ask them—remember, they're listening!), reassuring us that our instincts are correct. They may push us to forgive, to open our hearts, to release our guilt. But unlike Spirit Guides, they very rarely just flat out tell us what to do.

Loved ones also have the important role of helping us release the emotional blocks that prevent us from learning our lessons, such as guilt, shame, and regret.

My student Mike struggled with addiction for years. Like most addicts, he had relapsed several times on his path to healing, and this was something that brought him immense guilt, especially because his family had gone to great lengths to send him to expensive rehabilitation centers. When his recently deceased grandfather came through in one of our sessions, the first thing he said was, *I forgive you for being high at my funeral.* Mike immediately began to weep. He explained to me that the pain of losing his grandfather had caused him to relapse yet again, this time after several years of sobriety when everyone thought he was done with his addiction for good. No one else in the family knew that he had relapsed; he had pulled himself out of it and gotten back on track within days, having saved enough money to fund his own treatment that time. But Mike felt incredibly guilty for showing up to the funeral under the influence. It took me a minute to process this information, because like his living family members, I hadn't known Mike was still struggling to stay clean. But then his grandfather sent another message.

Let it go, Mike, he said, showing me a hand releasing its grip. *This time, you got back on the wagon right away. You found the help you needed on your own. You finally took responsibility for your addiction and I'm proud of you.* Mike knew it was time for him to release the guilt that was no longer serving him and deal with his addiction pragmatically. In the months that followed, he found that he was able to go much deeper in his therapy and group work to heal the root of his addiction.

It's also worth noting that when loved ones offer advice, it tends to be the sort of detailed, emotionally affirming advice that Mike's grandfather and Leigh's father offered. They want us to not sweat the small stuff, showing us the softer sides of life like forgiveness, acceptance, and gratitude. They understand the human experience as well as—actually, better than—we do, so they aren't judging us for our foibles; instead, they're trying to show us what they could not see when they were alive.

Beyond that, our loved ones like to remind us that when we reach out to them, they are listening. Part of their work is to help us come to terms with death itself. They do this by reminding us that they are always there and that, despite our flaws, we are doing an excellent job of learning our lessons in this life.

Sometimes loved ones appear again and again in our lives. It's almost like they're attached to us somehow, like part of their soul's work is to guide ours by their very presence. My great-grandmother Alessandra is like that. She immigrated from Italy to the United States and passed away when I was thirteen. It was around that time that my parents split up, which brought even more pain to me, my mother, and our family. It was such an out of control time for me; I had no sense of what was happening and felt like I was drowning. My dream of the car careening off the dock was coming true.

Perhaps my great-grandmother understood this, because when she died, she decided that part of her would stay on with me. From what I understand, she was super-spiritual, though I don't remember that part myself and only know because my mom has told me many times about their spiritual conversations. What I do remember of my great-grandmother is her sending me out to the garden to harvest basil and mint—two smells that remind me of her to this day. When other psychic mediums read me, they often pick up on rosaries, and when I hear that, I know they're referring to my great-grandmother because I have her rosaries on my bedpost. My great-grandmother's energy has always been very close to me; I feel her with me often. But in true loved-one fashion, she doesn't really instruct me in any specific way. (Unless I'm cooking Italian food, that is! In that case, she might chime in to tell me what I need to add for it to be just right.) Most of the time, her work is much simpler. Her steady presence reminds me that my soul is infinite, and that this lifetime is just a blip in my greater process. She reassures me around my mediumship work and comforts me when I feel alone.

Loved ones like my great-grandmother Alessandra are often at their own funerals, as well as other important events like births, holidays, and weddings they might have attended when they were living. I once read a woman, Laura, who had just gotten married a few weeks before. Her deceased mother came through to say, ***I was so glad I could walk you down the aisle.*** She showed me Laura carrying her on her back as she walked between the church pews in a wedding dress, holding her bouquet. Not knowing how to interpret this, I just blurted out, "You carried her. She says you carried her down the aisle." Laura was astonished. She explained that she'd hidden a locket with her mother's picture inside her bouquet, which she quite literally carried down the aisle with her.

Our loved ones are with us all the time. They're observing us, listening to us, and—if we pay close attention—reminding us of what we already know. They are integral members of our team, with an important role to play in our evolution.

And beyond that, talking with them can help us better connect with our Spirit Guides. Let me explain how this works.

Rising from Grief

Part of being human is grieving when our loved ones pass away. This is unavoidable. A great deal of our work in this world is to learn how to open our hearts to love. The depth of our grief brings that love into raw detail, showing us exactly how much love we've let in.

As I've written elsewhere, grief was a part of my portal into the world of psychic mediumship. Between my two living children I experienced pregnancy loss. Shortly after finding out I was pregnant, I dreamed I wouldn't make it to term. Still, I wasn't prepared for how hard pregnancy loss would be, and the experience colored my life for some time, in part because I never let myself grieve it fully. Several years later, when I was in the process of divorcing my first husband, his father passed unexpectedly. I'd married rather young and counted my in-laws as part of my own family. My father-in-law had been dear to me. I knew our relationship would change when I divorced, but I wasn't prepared to lose him entirely. As it happened, these two events took place simultaneously, bringing a new layer of grief to that already difficult period of time for my family. Yet I can say with certainty that the murky depths of that time were integral to my spiritual process. As difficult as it all was, experiencing that grief helped me immensely along my way.

That said, I understand there are depths of grief I have not experienced. I have not lost my parents or spouse, nor have I lost a living child, which I believe to be the single greatest pain a person can experience. I know this because I have had the honor of working with many bereaved parents. Theirs is a sorrow I don't wish to imagine. A grief like that is something one never gets over; instead, one gets through the most painful part of it, likely over the course of years, and then learns to live with what remains.

I recently did a reading for a family who lost their teenaged daughter Rachel to a rare brain cancer. They were friends of a friend, and I knew a little bit about their story but had not met them before. Initially, just Rachel's mother and brother were going to be on the Zoom call, because her father was very skeptical and didn't want to participate. As I provided details about Rachel's life that I would have no way of knowing unless I were truly in direct connection with her, her father came into view of the camera; it turned out he had been there the entire time. Both he and his wife became very emotional as Rachel shared her experiences with them: her feelings about them as parents throughout her short life, how she was observing everything from the Other Side, and her good wishes for their grief process.

A few weeks later I ran into our mutual friend at the gym. "I went over to their house last week, and they told me what you did for them was incredibly healing," she said. I explained that I hadn't done anything; I had merely transmitted the messages their daughter was waiting to give them. "Well, whatever you did, it helped a lot," she answered, sharing that Rachel's mother had cried and said, "I got to spend the afternoon with my daughter. I thought I'd never be able to do that again." Not long after that, Rachel's father contacted me to ask for another reading.

In a situation like that, our Guides are the ones facilitating these connections: Rachel's Guides, her parents' Guides, and mine as well. Our mutual friend's Guides were probably also in on the deal. Our Guides are doing this because they want us to have that heart-opening experience of feeling our grief and our love all at once. This blasts open any closed doors we may have put on our heart during the intense grieving process. That sense of being in our loved one's presence gives us such an emotional experience. It's almost like a lucid dream, and it's undeniable.

Even when we didn't have a great relationship with someone when they were alive, contacting them on the Other Side relaxes us. This is because we learn that their life review has allowed them to see the bigger picture and drop their worldly woes.

I once read a young man named Saul whose mother had passed away. He was regretful because, in life, their relationship had been fraught; in fact, prior to her death, they hadn't spoken for years. He sensed her presence around him often, but wasn't exactly sure why she was there. As Saul told me all this, his shoulders began to tighten, rising up toward the sky like he was anticipating a blow. Though he didn't say it aloud, I intuited that he was worried she was disappointed in him and, like many others I'd read, thought she might be haunting him somehow.

When Saul's mother came through, she reassured him that she was pleased with how his life was progressing and that she, too, had felt very badly about the relationship they'd had when she was living. She had come to understand much more about her own role in the negativity between them in death and was at peace with it. She wished the same peace for him. ***I am with you, watching you,*** she said, ***but only because I want the very best for you.*** I watched as Saul's shoulders softened toward the floor.

Communicating with our loved ones helps us heal our grief. Healing grief usually does not mean we stop missing the person we lost or feel grateful for their death. I get really riled up when I see so-called spiritual messages that suggest this is a goal, or even a possibility, because a significant portion of the people I've had the honor of working with carry grief that is simply too immense for that. In many cases, the most we can ask for is to get through the worst of our grief, surviving however we possibly can, and then learn to live with it. Yet living with grief carries its own spiritual power. We begin to see the lessons we have learned through loss and grieving, understanding that these lessons are part of our work in this lifetime. We find ways to put those lessons into service, sharing them with the world around us in ways we find meaningful.

This healing process brings us out of the denser, heavier vibration of grief and into the higher frequencies. Experiencing dense and heavy vibrations is by no means unspiritual, and in the vast majority of cases, there is no way to love-and-light your way out of these heavy feelings, nor is there value in doing so.

I often think of a sign I saw at a hairdresser's that said "We Fix Bad Haircuts!" because on the psychic level, that's what I do: I fix bad readings. A whole lot of these bad readings have suggested that people are grieving incorrectly. A dear friend of mine went for a reading after she lost her dog, whom she really considered a part of her family; her dogs are her babies. The psychic she saw suggested that because of her grief, her dog was unable to fully pass on to the Other Side. The psychic implied that she was holding the dog here, or in some sort of limbo, by grieving him so hard. My jaw hit the floor. How absurd!

I want to be very clear with you, just as I was with her: there is no such thing as grieving too hard. We simply aren't able to hold others back from their process on the Other Side. Sometimes, someone's own regret about their life can hold them back, but nothing we do—not the relationship we had with them when they were living nor the way we grieve them when they die—is holding anyone else in this realm.

Still, the process of moving through those denser wavelengths and finding something higher is powerful and important. It's often a long and difficult road. It takes however long it takes, with our sorrow reaching whatever depths it needs to reach. We are not in charge of that. Our best work is to just grieve, however we do, and wait to be lifted to that new level: the one where we live with it.

That's when we reach the higher frequencies of love and light. It's not through will or determination or denial; it's through the gift of time and the act of showing up, repeatedly, for the love that underpins our pain. Doing so has a sort of cleansing effect on our being. It sets us on a new path, on which we can reach higher frequencies. And it's on those higher frequencies—when we are able to reach them, in our own time and as we are guided—that we can receive the even greater navigation services our Guides can offer us.

Creative and Informal

As I've worked with hundreds of people over the years, I've seen again and again that as we practice speaking with our loved ones on the Other Side, we become very comfortable. Even skeptics like Rachel's father open up over time. And then it's just like chatting with that person when they were alive. We're comfortable because we know the person we're speaking to. This is even more powerful when we start making contact ourselves, inviting the voice of our loved one into our everyday life.

Communicating with the loved ones we knew in this lifetime allows us to practice the type of comfortable, familiar, chatty back-and-forth that we will eventually use to connect with our Guides. This style of communication is simply easier to do with people we knew in the flesh. It feels less sticky and strange. I always encourage my students to speak with their Guides like they'd speak with family, but many are reluctant to do so, preferring a more formal, ceremonial connection. While I understand the desire to honor our Guides with pomp, I think they're far less uptight than most of us expect them to be, and we can really just chat them up like family or dear friends. Practicing with our actual family and dear friends on the Other Side helps us understand what that might look like.

It also helps us to practice looking for signs from our loved ones. Loved ones and Guides send us signs all the time! Yet it's often easier to receive them from loved ones because we are less likely to second-guess ourselves.

These signs can take all forms. Spirit is creative and can use anything available to signal to us—even technology! I told you in the last chapter about how, in the throes of the end-of-life decisions for Phoenix, I received the Field of Dreams card. Seconds after I pulled the card, a rain cloud passed over my house. It was one of those sudden, small showers that happen on a sunny day, which was uncommon for my area at that time of year. I suddenly knew it was my friend Diana, herself a psychic who had recently passed due to cancer, trying to send me a sign. Before she had passed we had agreed that Diana would send us all rainbows from the Other Side, and our psychic friends loved to share how we found them in the most unexpected places. So I hurried out of my house expectantly, looking for the rainbow I knew she would send.

I looked up and waited and waited some more. Eventually I had to admit my rainbow hadn't come, so I slumped back inside, feeling both dejected and confused.

I walked back over to the table where I'd left my phone and found a message from my and Diana's mutual friend. Of course, it was a picture of a rainbow she'd just seen outside her own house, miles away from my own. I texted back, "Diana is such a show-off!" and then explained what had happened.

Spirit loves to play these games with us. Our loved ones, like our Guides, take great joy in being playful and light. It's our job to meet them there by being equally informal in response.

When we're deep in grief, it can be hard to receive signs directly from our Guides. Because the vibration of grief is low, we can't connect with the messages they have for us. Yet Guides and loved ones will often send us signs like this, through others. I've read for many people who long to meet their loved one in a dream. Often these people are hurt to hear that the people around them are dreaming of this same loved one, when they aren't. This is still their loved one trying to reach them, though—the fact that the other person told them about the dream is proof that their loved one is trying to get through.

It's important to remember that our loved ones in Spirit are often learning the ropes, just like we are here on this physical plane. It can take some time for them to figure out how to get through to us. By working with them in this process, we learn to not take it all so seriously. We can relax and just let Spirit do their work.

The messages from Spirit will always find their way. A few weeks after we moved into our rental, where the Spirit of the owner I call Grandpa hangs out in the basement, the porch light stopped turning off.

It was bizarre. I knew which light switch to use and it had always worked before! But again and again, I'd switch it on and off, on and off, and it would just stay on. Finally, I decided to just unscrew the light bulb because it was driving me nuts. I walked up to the porch, reached my hand inside the glass shade and unscrewed it just enough so that it would stay in place without receiving electricity. It stayed off for several days.

Then one night my husband and I returned from an outing to see the light on again. I just sat there in the passenger seat, staring. I knew at that point it was some sort of sign.

The next day, I started to hear my ex-husband's father—the one who had died suddenly—telling me to text his wife. I hadn't heard from him in some time and wasn't in good touch with my former mother-in-law, so it felt completely random to reach out. Usually, I'd pass on a message like this easily, but I just didn't feel comfortable so I ignored him all day as he got louder and louder.

That night I had a dream. I was in my ex-husband's parents' house trying to fix a light, but I couldn't manage to do it. Then my former father-in-law walked in, so I asked him, "Are you going to fix this already?" "No," he answered, "tell her to fix it. Tell her to fix it. Tell her to fix it . . ." his words echoed over and over before fading away.

I woke up remembering the dream, but still feeling annoyed that I would have to break through my own awkwardness to reach out to my former mother-in-law. But then, all day, he nagged at me: ***Tell her about the dream.***

Finally, I broke down and sent her a text describing it.

She answered immediately—no awkwardness to be found. "The light on my front porch isn't working. It's been off for days. What are you psychic or something?"

I texted back: "My porch light isn't working right either!" I explained how I'd tried to unscrew it, but it still came back on. She agreed it was strange.

I didn't hear anything more until the next day, when she texted me to say her porch light had suddenly started working again and turned on. It's as if her husband were reminding her, ***I'm here!***

This is how creative Spirit can be. Our loved ones will set up these elaborate scenarios to remind us they're around. They'll mess with us; they'll come through friends and family; they'll do whatever they can. And they're incredibly informal about it. They're just as comfortable with us in death as they were when we knew them in life—sometimes, even more so!

When we work with our loved ones in this informal, comfortable way, we're reminded that we can behave the exact same way with Spirit too. This is crucial practice for our work with our Spirit Guides, and in the process, it helps us rise out of our grief and onto the higher frequencies. That's when our connection to our Guides really takes off. Suddenly, our journey with Spirit sprout wings.

EXERCISE:
WALK WITH ME

Let's take our meditation off the cushion and out on the road! Of course, if you have mobility limitations, you are welcome to adapt this exercise however works for you.

For this exercise, you'll need about twenty minutes and a relatively quiet street or path to walk. The beach also works well—this is one of my favorite places to walk. It's also best to put your phone on silent for this exercise, if you can. That said, Spirit is very creative in how they get through to us. That means any person, place, or thing you pass, any interruption, and even messages you receive on your phone can contain signs from your loved ones. While it's good to practice withdrawing a bit, pay close attention to any interruptions that occur.

Before starting your walk, take a moment to connect with yourself by closing your eyes, touching a tree, feeling your feet on the ground, taking a conscious breath, or doing anything else that seems appropriate for you. Then ask your loved one to join you on the walk.

Start walking. Don't worry about focusing too hard on your loved one, but be aware of your thoughts and don't let them drift too far. You may or may not feel your loved one arrive right away, and their presence may be subtler than you are expecting. Your thoughts may drift despite your efforts until they get to a point at which your loved one can come in. Just allow your thoughts to land on that person whenever and however they do.

When you feel them arrive, start by greeting your loved one informally. ("Hey!" "Hi!" or "Ooh, I've missed you!" will do.) Then start chatting with them in your mind as you would aloud when they were alive. Talk about what's happening in your life. Ask them what they think of what's new—your job, partner, friend, outfit, whatever. Tell them what you miss about them. See what they wish to share with you—perhaps moments when they stood at your side without your knowing or things they learned as they passed over. You can ask open-ended questions if you like (I suggest avoiding yes-or-no questions) and see what they say. Be informal, be free, and enjoy the time together.

When you finish your walk, thank them and give a short goodbye—make sure it's more like a "see you later" than something formal or stiff. Be creative and make it your own! You may see yourself hugging or kissing your loved one or squeezing their hand. Whatever way you would say goodbye in real life will suffice. Then, notice their energy slowly fading away from you.

You can return to this exercise anytime for any of your loved ones.

Chapter 5
CONSTRUCTION ZONE

IT'S INCREDIBLY EXCITING TO ESTABLISH AN ONGOING RELATIONSHIP with our Guides. Connecting with the spiritual guidance available to us is a game-changer. It shifts our whole perspective on reality.

At the same time, many of us have noticed that life and all of its messiness are still in the way. *We* are still in the way. Challenges still crop up in our daily life, and we find ourselves turning to the same old habits and knee-jerk responses far more often than we'd like. Our mind and ego are as present as ever. As much as we want to live in love and light, horns are still honking in bumper-to-bumper traffic; our tech devices are still crashing at the exact wrong moment; we still find ourselves caught up in petty disagreements; and other daily stresses abound. Most of us find ourselves sinking into a low vibration from the "little stuff" more often than we want to. Understanding our soul's greater plan doesn't always make the "big stuff" much easier, either; we still resist heartbreak and disappointment, cycle through the same struggles repeatedly, and have trouble seeing our very hardest challenges as opportunities for growth. It seems like everything has changed, but also like it hasn't. What's going on?

As spiritual beings, there are many tools available to us—including modern psychological techniques. I am not a psychologist, but on a personal level, I am a practitioner of many of these tools. I don't see them as separate from my spirituality. Rather, I find that working with psychology allows me to avoid spiritual bypassing, bringing my Guides into other aspects of my personal development work so they can help to show me the way.

This chapter is all about that process. Here, I'll show you how to find where our reactions originate so we can deconstruct and reconstruct them from their very foundations with our Guides at our side. This work is for everyone—including me.

Facing Our Deepest Work

A couple of years ago, I was invited to a weekend-long event that included some really well-known psychic mediums and intuitives. Though part of me felt nervous to be in such a setting, I was reassured by the fact that a good friend had invited me. She knew almost everyone else there and would introduce me to many of the professionals I respected, providing a cushion for my lingering concern that I wasn't quite good enough to be considered one of them.

This concern wasn't new, by the way. I'd been working on dealing with impostor syndrome for years, and I'd been discussing it with my Guides at length in recent months as I faced all the not-good-enough stuff that was coming up with the house sale and the changes in my body. I knew the opening night dinner would be a challenge for my ego, but I was ready.

The first activity was drinks and appetizers. My friend and I walked around the room talking to people, and I felt my self-esteem rise as she introduced me to the others. I was surprised by how kind and personable everyone seemed—though I was intimidat*ed*, no one was outright intimidat*ing*. Everything was going great.

Then, just before we sat down to dinner, my friend got a text. She looked up and smiled at the group, explaining that she couldn't stay for dinner and she'd meet up with the rest of us in the morning. My eyes widened as I realized I'd be sitting at the "cool kids' table" without her. She flashed me a look that seemed to say, "Don't you dare leave, MaryAnn. You've got this," before striding out the door.

As soon as we all sat down, I felt my body shrink in my chair. I tried to force my shoulders back and my spine straight, breathing deeply, but inside I was curled up into a ball. I was sure my discomfort was obvious, likely even more so because I was surrounded by a group of highly attuned intuitives. *Do they know?* I wondered, and then caught myself. *Of course they know; they're psychics. What are you even doing here, MaryAnn?* Everyone continued to be really friendly and welcoming, which shook me even further. I was painfully aware of the fact that this wasn't about *them*—it was completely, 100 percent about *me*. My Guides were working through the others to make that clear. Yet I still felt apologetic about my presence, as if I were crashing their party.

"Help!" I pleaded rather desperately to my Guides. But their response was simple: *You aren't intruding. You're meant to be here, and you're ready for this. Are you going to sit there and be uncomfortable or not sit there at all?*

I knew what I had to do. I stayed put.

I watched myself awkwardly order what the person next to me ordered—something I didn't even want to eat. I listened as I made neutral statements that betrayed nothing about my personality, attempting to keep up with the conversation without revealing anything that could leave me more vulnerable. The whole thing felt so cringe.

On another level, I knew my Guides had been preparing me for that moment, helping me work though my imposter syndrome for over a decade—ever since I'd first started charging money for readings. I couldn't deny that my issue was ego-driven. As I'd been growing my career, I'd sat down with celebrities, TV executives, and others as my Guides coached me through recognizing my worth. I'd learned to stand on my own two feet, to face those situations with total confidence and a smile to boot—after all, it was business. That's why my Guides had brought me to this particular challenge round, confronting my ego with the very people whose books I'd read, whose podcasts I'd listened to, and whose oracle decks I used regularly. Though the others were inviting me in as an equal, all I felt was that I didn't belong. The more they smiled at me and welcomed me into the conversation, the more I shrank away. And as agonized and awkward as I felt, I had to hand it to my Guides for their ingenuity. The absurdity of my resistance made it obvious that the whole thing had been divinely orchestrated.

Somehow, I made it through dinner and got back to my hotel room. As I got ready for bed, I reflected on how perfectly lovely everyone had been to me—including my Guides, who were probably laughing hysterically at my awkwardness. I wanted to be in on the joke. So I sat on the bed in my pajamas, grounded and cleansed myself, and got to work. "OK, guys," I said internally. "What's up?"

First, my Guides reminded me that part of my role is to teach, and part of teaching requires me to reach as many people as I can—which means I *have* to keep reaching high, no matter how intimidating I find the process. *We're going to make it tough,* they explained, *because you're ready for tough. It's time to get to the heart of what this is all about.* I offered a slightly pitiful wailing sound in response. But then I relaxed. "OK," I accepted. "I guess I'm ready."

That's when I started to dig. What was it about the situation that felt so totally high school? As soon as I had that thought, my Guides zoomed me back into my high school cafeteria. I saw myself at my usual lunch table, "the cool kids' table," and felt how deeply I'd doubted whether I belonged there. I remembered how I'd look toward the other girls and wish I could be as pretty, fashionable, and well-liked as they were.

My Guides showed me how over time, this feeling of discomfort started to morph into a sense of competition. I was on the basketball team, and there, my insecurity manifested as a strong desire to win. I'm not talking about the joy of exceeding a personal best—I wanted to beat the other team to prove I was enough. By the time I was a young adult working in retail sales, my insecure mind was full of competitive thoughts. I had to sell more, be more, do more. I had to work at the flagship store, get the promotion, and look my best all at once. Though I was outwardly warm and friendly to others, inwardly I was suffering. Then I saw myself again at the cringy dinner and almost laughed out loud—no longer sixteen, now fifty-four, and dealing with the same old stuff. And I knew I was truly ready to be done with it.

I sat there on the hotel bed, looking at my life in retrospect, and let myself fully experience a familiar set of feelings I loved to avoid: inadequacy, not-enough-ness, failure. Though I had been working with these feelings for a long time, it was the first time I really let them pass through me completely. Something deep was finally healing.

Before closing my meditation, I asked my Guides to send some sort of sign to show me that I wasn't wrong—that this was, indeed, a huge moment in my evolution. And then I released the feeling, knowing it would be done. As I crawled under the covers, I let out a deep sigh and fell asleep grateful.

Asking *Where Did This Start?*

The type of insecurity I was facing may or may not be familiar to you. Yet its base, ego, is something every human on a spiritual path is bound to face. Ego is the one that tells us we're separate from the rest—that we're better or worse than the others. Sometimes ego tells us to play it small, so we don't get disappointed. Other times, it tells us to push ourselves beyond our limits to ensure we don't end up with second place. Ego is a tricky little bitch, and every time we think we've caught it, it shows up in a new way. Whenever ego shows up for me, I know my Guides are leading me to tame it so I can truly serve others. Spirit doesn't want me to be better or worse than anyone else—instead, they want me to be my best *and* support others at the same time. This way, we can all contribute our very highest gifts to the world.

So where did my ego pick up its nasty habits? This is an important question for anyone grappling with ego to ask themselves, because it forces us to seek out where our habits started: namely, the challenges we experienced early in life that still govern our behavior today.

So where did my ego pick up its nasty habits? This is an important question for anyone grappling with ego to ask themselves, because it forces us to seek out where our habits started: namely, the challenges we experienced early in life that still govern our behavior today.

When one of my best friends started diving deep into her childhood through therapy, my Guides suggested I ask her about it. I started peppering her with questions about what she was learning and how she was processing it all. Our Guides will always lead us to the modalities and methods that can help us, and as soon as my friend explained the work she was doing, I knew it could help me.

My friend described how she would mentally travel back to some of the more painful moments of her early life to try to gain understanding of how she developed some of the habits and beliefs that had come to hold her back as an adult. Then she would talk to her younger self, using a simple conversational method to shift how she felt about those events today. Even though I was new to these ideas, we immediately began discussing the power and importance of bringing our Guides into this other work. The trauma work she was describing was very much about this one single incarnation, but it was clear to both of us that bringing Guides along could offer safety and context to enhance the experience. I'd already been doing similar work through visualization, automatic writing, etc., but I adapted what she'd told me and started directly conversing with my younger self.

I began with something that felt very ripe for me: the concerns about self-worth that had come up around moving. I sat down on my living room sofa, closed my eyes, and questioned my Guides about where those feelings came from. I asked, "Where did this start?"

Immediately, they brought me back to the many times I'd moved in the years after my parents' divorce. They showed me how the idea of packing boxes and moving was therefore associated in my young mind with fear, instability, and the vast unknown. I sat in my home as an adult, refeeling everything I'd felt as a child.

I longed for a so-called "normal" family like so many of my friends had, with two parents, a stable homelife, large family vacations, and the like. More than that, I longed for a physical home I could rely on, and I desperately wanted the stability that I imagined came with living in just one place. My Guides sent me images and feelings all at once, like a flash flood; part of me was sitting on my sofa in the house I was reluctant to sell, and part of me was a heartbroken little kid.

I started having a conversation, allowing these two parts to come together for a chat.

"What would you have me know?" I asked the child in me.

"I don't like feeling unstable all the time. I want to feel OK wherever I am," the child answered.

"How can we do that?"

She thought hard, and then said, "Let's just be OK. Let's just be OK wherever we are."

I smiled. I could do that. I could do it right now. I saw my adult self reaching down and hugging the child in me. "OK. I promise. We'll be OK wherever we are." I asked my Guides for a sign to remind adult me, as well as the little child within, that things were OK.

A few weeks later, my husband and I listed the house. We got a great offer immediately. Midway into the negotiation process I started to see hummingbirds around me regularly. I realized this was my sign from my Guides. Hummingbirds would appear as I packed up things to sell or donate; they would zoom by when I was on the phone with the realtor; they hovered outside the window as I told a friend we'd signed the paperwork. Sometimes, the little girl in me would take the wheel, and I'd find myself lamenting how unfortunate it was that we were moving. At each one of those moments, a hummingbird would arrive as if to say, *Hey. We're OK, remember?* This would allow me to get back into the driver's seat.

At the same time, I was doing similar work around my insecurity. As I wrote before, impostor syndrome wasn't new to me; my Guides had been chattering at me about it for some time. Yet in the months leading up to the painfully awkward dinner I'd started asking my Guides, "Where did this start?" That one simple question sent the work into overdrive.

My Guides showed me myself as a young teenager, fighting with my first boyfriend. Things had started out OK, but over time he became increasingly emotionally abusive. He was manipulative, jealous, and would often say negative things about my body, which I internalized. He frequently compared me to his ex-girlfriend and said he thought she was prettier, skinnier, and better than me in every way. This early experience of "romance" had a profound effect on my self-esteem. Long after we broke up, and even once I'd realized how abusive his behavior was, deep down I carried the belief that I wasn't worthy of anything better.

Through my meditation I invited the young adolescent version of me into the conversation, with our Guides surrounding us. She explained, "I'm getting my self-worth from him, and he's telling me I'm not worth that much at all." She showed me how this pivotal young relationship had created a hole in my self-esteem. My Guides took over then, showing me other moments from my relationship history. Though the relationships I had in the years that followed were healthier, I saw that I continued to people-please for a long time, trying to prove my worth to the men who already loved me. As I ended the meditation, I couldn't deny that this one early experience had really left its mark on me. I realized I had deep work to do on my self-esteem.

My Guides proceeded to show me some methods I could use to do it—one of which is at the end of this chapter. Over the months that followed, I found myself journaling, visualizing, doing automatic writing, and using every tool available to me to feel securer in myself. This prepared me for the deep release that was coming for me in the hotel room after the dinner.

Getting through challenges like these isn't one-and-done; it takes time and work. We chip away at the ego little by little. It's hard, but incredibly rewarding. The more I've done this work, the more I've come to understand that it isn't detracting from my spiritual life—it's adding to it. The challenges I faced early on, like bouncing from house to house and that first relationship that hurt me so deeply, are reflections of the lessons I came here to learn. I *needed* those issues to come up to embody the confident, stable, supportive being I came here to be.

That doesn't mean we deserve what happened to us, whatever it may be. This is an important distinction that deserves some unpacking of its own.

Our Own Construction Zone

I've focused much of this chapter on my own process because it's the one I know best, and it's *great* for my ego to have to be so publicly vulnerable. But I feel somewhat tender about writing about these early experiences and how they affected me, because I know that plenty of people have gone through far worse than I did. My parents always loved me and never mistreated me; they just had to do what was right for them. Yes, I had a bad first boyfriend, but the relationships that followed were mostly good for me overall. In contrast, you or someone you know may have experienced abuse, severe mistreatment, or very real scarcity of something essential like food, shelter, safety, or love. Many of us have lived through truly heartbreaking realities that go far beyond what I have experienced in this lifetime.

It's important to understand that no matter what any of us have had to deal with, none of us needed or deserved the exact sequence of events that occurred. I don't see fate as a predetermined set of external experiences; free will is involved, too, and there are plenty of bad actors (and bad actions) at play when it comes to how people are hurt in this world. What I believe *is* predetermined is the internal experience: the set of feelings that came up when these events took place.

In other words, my parents' divorce was not precoded on my soul. What was precoded was becoming overly attached to outer stability, because that is a major part of what my soul came to overcome in this lifetime. The bad boyfriend wasn't precoded either; the insecurity that followed is what was. This is true for all of us, regardless of what we face. Your soul may have called you to experience *something* that would bring up feelings of being not good enough, not deserving love, or believing that the world is not a safe place, for instance. These are a direct reflection of what your soul came here to learn: that you are wonderful exactly as you are, that you deserve all the love in the world, and that you embody the safety you may have not received. Our souls evolve through these feelings; the emotions and the beliefs they build within us are our construction zone, not the experiences themselves.

Consider my student Britt, who was blessed with a spiritual awakening in her midfifties. Britt had spent years as an overachiever. She had an impressive résumé that had taken her to the top of a travel company. She then sold her company for millions and went on to be a successful keynote speaker and author. She had a happy family, a beautiful home in the suburbs, and even a vineyard in the Italian countryside. Between professional positions she had pushed herself as an equestrian show jumper, working with beautiful horses she had begun to breed. It seemed like everything she touched turned to gold—her life seemed, from the outside, *perfect*.

Yet at some point she started to realize that her dedication to success was looking less like an accomplishment and more like a spiritual hindrance. Britt felt an emptiness she could not fill—not with a number in her bank account, not with her children's accomplishments, not with a blue ribbon or a trophy. That word *perfect* turned her stomach. It felt like more of a curse than a blessing.

Seeking answers, she went to a series of ceremonies with a shaman who was serving the psychedelic medicine ayahuasca. She spent her first night purging her body and her second confronting her own death. As Britt continued, she got in touch with memories of abuse from childhood that she hadn't allowed herself to face. In her third ceremony, she met a Guide who helped her connect the fear she'd had as a child when she could not control what was happening to her body with her quest for perfection in adulthood. For the very first time in her life, she understood the interplay between perfection and control. The Guide showed her herself as a little girl screaming, "I can't be perfect anymore! I don't want to be!" This experience left her shaking.

Britt went home from the third ceremony grateful for what ayahuasca had given her and certain that her work was far from over. In the months that followed, she continued to sit with the Guide she had met in meditation. This Guide led her to understand more about how her unresolved feelings were still affecting her life in the present. It showed her when it was time to bring her memories of abuse to her family and how to navigate their reactions. Eventually, it helped her release some of her perfectionism and embrace the beauty of her personal drive in a way that promoted her overall well-being. She started intentionally practicing releasing control and began to do things imperfectly by design. She played with clay and paint, even though she wasn't very "good" with either, and lost herself for hours. She sang karaoke off-key. She made a practice of failure, and she loved it. In doing so, Britt found a more peaceful balance between manifesting and allowing, measuring her success by a wider set of metrics.

Britt learned to be grateful for what she had made from healing her abuse—she didn't become grateful for the abuse itself. It's an important distinction. She understood that she came here to work through trying to be perfect—a battle she was always going to lose—so she could truly embrace and love herself as she is.

Today, Britt coaches other successful practitioners through what she calls "joyful experimentation." Her top clients are perfectionists and self-described "control freaks" who have forgotten how to enjoy *doing* because they're so focused on *achieving*. With the Guide she met during the ayahuasca ceremony at her side, Britt helps her clients find the inner happiness they were seeking all along.

Britt's story shows us that two important things happen when we do this work. First, we find the thing our younger self truly wants from us: most often, the exact opposite of the annoying habit we're embodying as an adult. Second, it helps us pay that forward. Let's take a look at how that works.

A Game of Opposites

Our life story can give us loads of information if we choose to look at it like an instruction manual for unlocking our soul. It isn't easy to work on the same thing over and over again, but when we see it happening, we can know for certain that we've landed on one of the most important things we came here to learn.

Once we've connected with our Guides to figure out where our patterns start and conversed with our younger selves to understand how they interpreted challenging experiences, we get to the final stage of the process: finding the flip side of our challenges and eventually discovering a way to pay that flip side forward.

Britt did this by releasing her need to control, embracing her imperfection, and helping others do the same. As I work with my sense of instability around moving, I've sought to feel OK wherever I am and then pass that sense of true inner stability on to my friends, students, and everyone I meet. Throughout the process of selling our home, I'm reminding members of my family that we're totally OK, we're resilient in the face of change, and we'll continue to feel stable wherever (and whenever!) we land again. Of course, as I'm telling them, I'm telling myself—the work is never over, though it gets deeper and richer as we go.

In the time I've been working with impostor syndrome, I've made great strides. I've developed an incredible group of friends who provide one another with personal and professional support. I've encouraged others to develop their gifts through my work as a medium mentor. I've thrown myself wholeheartedly into the pursuit of our mutual success.

That's part of why it was so frustrating to see my impostor syndrome on full display the night of the dinner. But in truth, it was just proof that dealing with feeling like I'm not enough is some of my greatest work. The morning after my impostor syndrome took over, I had another opportunity to see my hard work reflected back to me.

As I walked into the conference hall, I encountered a psychic medium who had been on my radar for years. I'd long admired her and was struck by her kindness and the welcoming feeling she'd given me throughout the previous evening. She immediately offered up a kind smile, her eyes almost piercing mine. Then she looked around to see if anyone else was listening. Seeing that our conversation would be private, she raised her eyebrows and asked quietly, "Who are you to think you shouldn't be here?" She said it in a no-nonsense, almost stern tone, like the one my Guides use when they're pushing me. "Stop that. You deserve to be here."

I broke into a wide grin. I'd been caught! I was certain this was the sign my Guides had promised was coming—she even sounded like them! I laughed and said, "Yeah, I'm still working on that one. What are you—psychic or something?"

"You'll get there," she reassured me, switching back into her usual warm persona. We took our chairs. I spent the rest of the weekend feeling like I belonged, like I deserved to be there, like I was a true equal.

That's the thing about our Guides: they show up in the most amazing ways. They'll throw us to the wolves sometimes, like at the dinner, but they'll also give us hummingbirds when we need them. They know when to be delicate and when to be harsh. Their only goal is to help us evolve so that we can spread light and love in the world.

When we really do our work, sharing light and love isn't spiritual bypassing—it's the highest offering there is. Getting curious about our behavior and starting to recognize what we came here to learn make us accountable for what no longer serves. And choosing that accountability has a profound effect on our development. We can't just say we want to heal. We have to be willing participants, and we have to open ourselves to the work with gratitude.

The following exercise will help you do precisely that.

EXERCISE: WRITE AND RELEASE

Start by cleansing yourself. Then sit quietly for a few moments, feeling yourself root down into the earth.

Next call your Guides to sit around you. You may or may not be able to see their individual faces; what is most important is just that you feel their presence. You can say aloud, "I call upon my Guides to support me," or any version of that statement that resonates with you.

When you feel your Guides have arrived, consider the issues you're dealing with in your life today. Notice the themes that come up. For instance, you may notice *financial insecurity, issues with body size, distractibility/trouble paying attention, worry, focusing on the negative, ruminating on the past, gossip,* etc. There are simply too many themes to list here, so be creative and believe whatever your Guides tell you. Write each theme that arises on its own piece of paper—it could just be one, or as many as ten.

When that's complete, sit with the piece(s) of paper in front of you. Ask, "Where did this start?" Let your Guides take you back in time to show you the answers. Have a chat with the younger version of yourself.

Whenever your Guides show you a particular person or experience that triggered that theme in you, imagine handing the paper over to that person or surrendering it to the experience. See yourself handing the theme back, without anger or resentment, but simply because it isn't serving you anymore.

When you have completed all the steps for each piece of paper, find a way to safely burn them, either in a metal container or over the sink. (Make sure you have good ventilation, low wind, and water handy!) You can also release them into water or dramatically tear them up over the trash can—find the symbolic act that works for you. Keep your Guides at your side as you let go of what doesn't serve you. It's not over, but already you've taken a huge step.

This may be enough for today. If that's the case, you know what's best for you. Just promise me—and yourself—that you'll come back to the final steps that follow.

When you're ready, start to ask yourself how you can flip it around. How could you transform your challenge into its opposite? If you struggle with greed, how could you become more generous? If you've worked on needing to be right, how might you embrace defeat and admit when you're wrong? If you're prone to feeling abandoned, how could you trust that you will be held and supported?

And then, ask your Guides to help you in paying it forward. Embody the very trait that has been so hard for you to achieve. Show up for the people around you with the very thing you lack. It's a subtle but extremely important way to calm your ego and live your spiritual truth—one that doesn't rely on bypassing, but on directly confronting our spiritual lessons and turning them into gifts for the world.

You may need to repeat this exercise several times. Don't worry—that's proof that you've found one of your deepest lessons. Remember to always ask your Guides for support, because they are the very best allies you have in this process. You're never alone in this; in fact, you have an entire team cheering for you.

Chapter 6
ARE WE THERE YET?

AS WE TRAVEL THIS ROAD WITH SPIRIT, WORKING ON THE challenges we've faced in this lifetime is imperative. These challenges are arising to show us something greater about our soul: the lessons we come here to learn reflect our stage in the process on a wider level.

This means we are likely to experience the same lessons over and over again. If we could keep that in mind and zoom out to see the big picture, perhaps each of our challenges would be easier to face. It isn't that easy, though. We often want to keep barreling down the road toward an idealistic destination, and every stop along the way feels like it's holding us back. Ego hates this. It feels frustrating to have to pause again and again to face things we've confronted before. "*Waaahhhhhh!*" we whine. "Are we ever going to get there?"

One of the most important things to remember is there is no "there" for us to get to. Better yet, consider what "there" might be for you: a life without problems? An incarnation without lessons to learn? We're here to travel the path minute to minute. We could have booked a quick flight, but we wanted a road trip instead.

This feeling of "Are we there yet?" often escalates when we start working with our Guides. As we start to comprehend just how powerful they are, as well as how capable we are at connecting with them, we sometimes begin to harbor a feeling that they can solve all our problems. We hope that they won't just make life a little bit easier, but that they'll make it easy, period. After all, they can fix everything in the higher realms, right? This is certainly true for day-to-day annoyances but it becomes even more extreme with our biggest struggles, whatever they are—health, money, relationships, purpose, or the seeming inability to manifest a specific dream. It's easy to think that if we are just spiritual enough, if we cleanse ourselves regularly and talk to our Guides and meditate every single day, we'll break our way out of the cycle of lessons.

But here's the thing: ***this is life.*** This is what it's supposed to be about. It never really ends; the final destination you imagine is actually just a transition to something else. And lest you fall into despair about that, consider instead how that truth can actually free you. If we choose to surrender to the fact that we are always learning, our life can be so much more fulfilling. We are here within ourselves in each moment. When we put our feet up and enjoy the twists and turns, the road itself can become light and fun. There's a fantastic soundtrack and crunchy snacks and good company. And of course, there's a spectacular view.

Divine timing has much more in store for us than we could ever imagine. When we look back on things, we will have the opportunity to see how everything worked out with perfect rhythm and cadence, one step after the next after the next. Impatience suggests we know better than Spirit, but the truth is that everything rolls out right on time—always.

This chapter is all about dealing with that voice of impatience by embracing the divine timing that is taking place. We all struggle with this; no one is exempt, I promise! In this work, the goal isn't to shut that voice off, but rather to recognize it when it pipes up, hear it out, and soothe it with kindness and understanding. ***I know you want to get there,*** we can say with a smile, ***but that's not what we're here to do.*** Then turn up the music, throw your head back, and sing as loud as you can.

The Longest Road

Impatience is one of the biggest challenges we face as spiritual beings.

We often justify our impatience, saying, "Well, I really ***should be*** impatient to get rid of this or that bad habit," or "It's ***best*** to be impatient about things that aren't serving me." It could be easy to think it's a good thing to be impatient about our challenges because impatience will somehow push us through them, as if impatience itself were a motivating force. But this isn't the case. To the contrary, we are exactly where we are: with this or that bad habit, with those things that may not be serving us, with our challenges.

And when that is the case, it's ***impatience itself*** that we are being called to address and overcome.

Our impatience can take many forms. We can feel impatient while waiting for a certain situation to manifest in our external lives: a job, a relationship, monetary gain, etc. We can be impatient as we wait for our new house to be built or for our hormones to stop going haywire (who, me?!). The biggest form of impatience, however, is our impatience to ***get somewhere*** spiritually—which reinforces the false concept that there is anywhere to get to. The truth is that we're never done. There is no "graduating" from spiritual work on this plane. As long as we're here, the lessons are going to come; it's guaranteed. We are best served when we stop being frustrated by that and start focusing on how we can rise to respond to whatever comes our way.

I was once reading a room full of about 500 people at an advanced-level spiritual workshop. I wasn't mentoring or advising them; I was accessing the psychic realms to allow the Guides and loved ones in the room—the accumulated Guides and loved ones of all 500-plus people there—to come through. As so often happens, Spirit called me over to a particular person in the audience. I looked at him directly and asked into the microphone whether I could read for him. He had that half-happy, half-terrified look people often have when they're chosen for a reading: excited to have been selected but nervous about what their Guides and loved ones are going to say through me.

His sister began to speak through me. She first proved to him who she was by providing details I could have had no way of knowing. Then she lovingly shared that he still had work to do around grief and releasing things he had lost: a relationship, a job, and a friendship that was no longer as strong as he wished it to be. He teared up at this, showing just how deeply his sister's words were touching his heart. Since loved ones only confirm what we are already considering, I knew that on some level he was aware he had work to do in grieving these things. Yet I sensed some shame in him, as if he didn't want to hear he had to grieve—especially in front of his peers. Trying to lighten things up, I put his sister on hold and interjected that it wasn't the worst thing in the world to do more work, laughing a little as I joked that such work was the entire point of the spiritual workshop we were all attending. Yet I could tell it wasn't landing, so I gently ended the reading and moved on to the next person.

About a week later I received an emotional email from him. He was angry and hurt by the reading. He said he had felt humiliated when I laughed. As I read the email, I was taken aback; I had never meant to hurt him and was horrified that I had made his process any harder. I took a breath and then wrote him back, adding more interpretation to what I'd heard from his sister: yes, he had more work to do, but that didn't mean he hadn't done a good deal of work already. I explained that since he had grieved his sister's death so wholeheartedly, she was asking him to grieve the other losses in his life with the same attention and focus. "Grief is complex; it's ongoing," I wrote. "Your sister knows you can do this. She's seen you do it before. She's seen the depth and breadth of your heart, and she's calling you to stretch it once again."

It turned out he really had done a lot of spiritual work, because he was able to bring himself out of his anger, hurt, and shame to have a bigger conversation with me. It took a lot of courage on his part, and I was impressed! The email exchange that followed went on for months and became quite friendly, to the point that if we ever meet again in this life I'm sure we will both be glad for it.

I think his reaction perfectly encapsulates the knee-jerk response that most of us have when we are reminded that this trip isn't over. We're resistant; we're exhausted; we're devastated; we're terrified. We want to blame someone else or put it off or somehow "graduate" out of needing to do more work. Yet we are here to learn. Even those of us who are teachers are forever students.

It's common that we look to others and think, *They must not have to work as hard as I do.* We fall into the all-too-common trap of comparison and decide that someone else has it easier. Most of the time, when we look at others, we're working with incomplete information. We can never really know what someone else is going through or how hard their situation is. Sure, if someone is facing the tragic death of a loved one or a difficult diagnosis or their house burns down, we can see their suffering, but we can never really understand how something—even something that seems small—can be so entirely big to someone else.

That's part of why I'm sharing so openly about my personal challenges in this book: while on the outside they may seem to be surface-level, to me they're much deeper. I'm facing feelings of abandonment and existential dread, wild as that may be, because I'm moving; I'm facing terror, worthlessness, and being entirely out of control because my body is going through menopause. These things that may seem like no big deal to others are huge challenges for me, precisely because they touch on the greatest wounds still within me—the wounds I came here to heal. And pretty much everyone has challenges like that.

Yet it wouldn't be fair to deny that some people really do have it easier. Not always—all souls go through essentially the same process—but for parts of their lives, and even a whole lifetime, people can experience minimal drama and relatively painless lessons. It can be easy to resent them for that, especially when we're in a challenging moment or a flat-out challenging lifetime. Yet instead of responding with judgment or jealousy, we can instead simply observe and learn from each other. We can notice our own impatience to get to the good stuff, whatever that is.

This is harder to do when there seems to be a domino effect of negative or challenging experiences. Sometimes people experience hardship after hardship. A dear friend of mine is dealing with heart problems and has had to have numerous operations over the last few years. In that same time frame, her father has passed away and her husband is experiencing major challenges in his health. I understand how she's just getting hit after hit after hit, and as with so many other things, there isn't a way to bypass that; it just stinks all the way through. In her case, there may be no way to completely vanquish her impatience for things to get better; she has to feel her grief and deal with her health and be in this impossible phase of her life all at once. Yet this is simply what it is right now. She can use her free will to stay positive and get through it, looking for the highest spiritual lessons within the process, but she can't just wish away her pain.

In a situation like that, the very best we can do is to balance our own thoughts by acknowledging the good stuff, even if it's something simple. I'm talking incredibly simple here: a delicious peach on a restricted diet, a sunset while you're stuck in traffic, a kind nurse who finds the vein easily. Allowing these instances to bring us gratitude for even a moment during our struggle lets some balance on board. This is what gives us the patience we need to continue. It helps us keep our anxiety and fear at bay, knowing what is within our control—how we respond to the events in our life—even when we have zero control over the events themselves.

As we continue down this long road with a curiosity about our own impatience, we start to notice the themes that come up again and again in our work. These are the lessons we came here to learn.

Didn't We Already Get Past That?

In chapter 3 we looked at the idea of alternate timelines, which show us the many ways life could go depending on how we act with our free will. And in the previous chapter we considered that though it isn't encoded on our soul to have certain experiences, it is encoded for us to receive certain lessons. These lessons often come in stages; we learn as much as we can in each stage before moving on to the next. But in each stage, we come up against the lesson again, even when we think we conquered it before.

My student Julie came up against this when she got into a new relationship. During one of our sessions she explained how well things were going: the guy she was seeing wanted a long-term commitment—which she hadn't experienced in quite some time—and seemed to have his life together. I was excited for her because she had just come off a string of disappointing breakups. One guy had cheated on her; another had broken up with her to go back to his ex; and two more had not been willing to commit. In our next session I asked how it was going.

"It's OK, but he sends me some pretty heavy texts sometimes," Julie said with a sigh. She explained what she meant by "heavy": in one, he told her he loved her. In another, he said she was the woman of his dreams.

I was confused. What was wrong with that? "That doesn't sound too heavy," I said tentatively. "Maybe it's just sweet."

"Yeah, but it reminds me of what I've been through with other people. I feel like I've been here before, and I thought I'd manifested something different this time! I don't understand how my Guides can let me go through these same feelings again." She went on to talk about the difficult emotions she was experiencing around self-worth, fear, and cynicism. Ironically, these feelings from her past relationships were showing up in this new one no matter how much better it seemed to be.

I explained to Julie that there is no point in bringing the past into the present, but that if she doesn't like that kind of communications she was getting from him just yet, she can tell him. "I don't know . . . I feel like I already worked through these feelings," Julie explained as she started to cry. "I thought I would be ready for this. I didn't realize it would bring so much up for me, and I don't know how to reconcile that with all the work I've done."

Julie's challenges are surfacing in this new relationship with someone who really cares for her, just as they came up with partners who didn't value her enough, because they are just that: *her* challenges. It's clear to me that Julie came here to experience lessons around self-worth, fear, and cynicism. The men she dates just set those lessons into motion.

Our Guides know the greater lessons we are here to learn, just as they see the challenges we undergo in the process of learning them. They are fully aware of what it is we're going to experience in life—the good and the bad. They have walked with us before and know us very well. Their role, then, is not to spare us our challenges because those challenges are in service of our lessons. They understand the gravity of that, because many of them have experienced human life before, with their own set of challenges and lessons to learn. Yet their goal is to help us access our higher self amid our struggle and to help us trust in the process.

Often, our Guides bring us a repeated circumstance to show us just how far we've come. I experienced this recently myself when I came up against my self-worth stuff: insecurity, impostor syndrome, all that. The instability of being between homes, flying back and forth between Long Island and Florida as I close my residence in one location and shift it to the other, has brought these feelings on even more strongly. I have this sense that I don't know if I've progressed enough in life because I don't know where I belong.

Sometime last spring, I started to have flashes of an earlier time in my life: one when I was in a really bad relationship and living in a sad little apartment on what I'll call Cora Street. I felt like I was hearing the name Cora everywhere, and each time I'd play out some little scene from that time. I even had a dream about my life on Cora Street and the darkness I felt when I lived there.

Around that time a friend of mine was quite sick and on a medication that left her unable to drive, so different members of her inner circle took turns ferrying her to various medical appointments. I was excited by the opportunity to spend time together, so I signed up for one of the further-out appointments across Long Island. There was some sort of traffic jam that day, so the GPS took us a very roundabout way, rerouting us several times. I kept getting turned around; even after living here for over fifty years, I found myself confused as to where I was as we followed the labyrinthine course through neighborhoods and backstreets. It was weird enough that I knew my Guides were up to something. "What's going on, guys?" I asked, suspicious. Finally, I found myself at an intersection that looked eerily familiar.

Then my GPS dinged and chirped out, "Turn right on-to Co-ra Street," in its halting, robotic voice. I laughed out loud. We turned right and passed the very apartment complex where I had lived thirty years ago. Suddenly it all made sense.

When I lived on Cora Street, I was still grieving another relationship—bad enough grief that I'd gotten together with a really difficult person in response. I wanted to avoid how I felt; I wanted to prove that I was an adult, that I'd "gotten somewhere." And for months, I put up with all sorts of ridiculous behavior from my boyfriend. My self-esteem tanked in the process. I felt like an impostor, a kid living an adult life. Yet I wanted the stability of a long-term relationship. I wanted to keep things simple, to not have to pack up and leave, to not have to mend my heart and be single and start again. So I stayed.

Then one day we had yet another huge fight, and I heard, *Just leave.* I'd thought about leaving before, but I'd always made it really complicated. I didn't know how to pack everything up since we'd bought a lot of things together, and I generally just dreaded having to box my possessions up (a common theme, as you now know). The voice I heard then—the voice of my Guides—insisted it was actually quite simple. I realized I only needed a few nights' worth of clothes. I could abandon the rest forever, or I could even get it later, but I had to get out. *Just leave.*

Without thinking about it any further, I quickly packed a small bag of essentials. I don't think I even grabbed my toothbrush. I put my key on the table and walked out the door. Later, I sent a friend to pack the rest, and it turned out the whole process was much easier than I'd anticipated.

I remembered all of this in the block it took us to pass the apartment complex. *Don't you see how far you've come?* my Guides asked me. I thought about all that I have now: a stable and healthy relationship, a secure environment, beautiful grown kids, a solid career. I no longer rely on someone else to make me happy. I love being alive. And yet these same issues of insecurity, impostor syndrome, and fear of not being good enough remain. When my Guides took me down Cora Street, they showed me that these questions aren't indicative of where I am in life; they're reflective of my own fears.

When I was in my early twenties, I harbored a strong hope that I would have a simple and predictable life. Traditionalism, for me, was the highest goal. I had a career in retail fashion, and I thought I'd just climb that ladder to the top, taking an appropriate amount of time away to be with my kids and then jumping right back in. I thought I had to get into the right relationship young and stay in it for the long haul—so much so that I stayed in the wrong relationship for quite some time. The idea of owning one house forever and ever was a part of that greater dream. The challenges I faced in childhood led me to idealize lives that stayed the same and to fear the natural shifts that take place as evidence of personal failure. I wanted to be "good." I wanted to succeed. Somehow this idealized, traditionalist dream came to represent all of that.

It's taken until now for me to realize that my life is anything but simple or predictable. I've had three careers: the one in fashion, my years as a stay-at-home mom, and now this unexpected one as a psychic medium. I've had two major relationships since that one on Cora Street: one with my first husband and the father of my kids and the marriage I've been in for over a decade now with my forever love. I've had a lot of stability, but the only part of that traditionalist dream that ever really fit me was the time I spent home with my kids—years I loved so much, I extended them longer than I ever expected. Everything else about my life has just been more variable than that. Driving down Cora Street in my fifties has helped me embrace my true, authentic self, complete with all my phases. I've come to understand that I don't need to be "good" or achieve some externally verifiable success to be loved; I just need to be myself. Amid a little instability and all that brings, I have the opportunity to see that I've come so far. I believe in myself so much more than I once did. I'm so much more honest about who I am.

I've also come to see the value in having phases in life. When we don't aim to make everything last forever, we can experience many things, and each one of them can be awesome. It's like being Madonna: there are so many Madonnas, and they are all amazing. Lucky Star Madonna, Material Girl Madonna, Like a Prayer Madonna, Vogue Madonna, Cone Bra Madonna, Yoga Madonna, Ray of Light Madonna (obviously the best Madonna), Mom Madonna, and now sixty-something toned-arms still-killing-it Madonna. Each one is different and yet, like her or not, they're all authentically Madonna. We can all have that.

There are also a ton of benefits that come when we stop trying to predict the road ahead and get everything right. I didn't know what I wanted to do with my life early on, which made my traditionalist dream even harder to achieve. I would get down on myself because I didn't have a career that required a college education, and though I was really good at working in retail fashion, it wasn't something that I loved to do. I always felt not good enough because of that. When I had my first child, though, I understood completely why I didn't love my career. It was so easy to walk away from. I knew that my next phase was to be a mom—and I loved that. If I'd adored my career too, it would have been much more difficult to leave it behind.

So in truth, instability has served me in many ways. During a challenging time in my life, I have been guided to see how much more willing I am to move from one phase to another. *Look how far you've come,* my Guides say, and they're right: though it's hard for me, I'm embracing a little instability now. I'm jumping into the unknown in a way that I have rarely done before. I'm still shaky with it—it isn't easy, that's for sure. But I'm doing it anyway.

This is the way to respond when we find ourselves cycling back on the same lessons again and again. We are getting opportunities to encode the lesson on a deeper level. We are being offered the chance to really get it right—to heal the idealistic versions of ourselves that are holding us back and come home to the authentic selves that are here waiting for us. Doing so requires not only patience but also a belief in the greater plan for us: the story our soul is here to live.

Your Soul's Story

Up to this point, I've made plenty of references to past lives and incarnations and souls. It's time to take a deeper look at how that all works together. And more importantly, *why* it does.

Each of us has a much greater mission than we can ever understand in this single lifetime. We have lived many times before, and we will continue to live many, many times. In the space between lives, we choose when to incarnate again and what specific lessons we will learn during that time—and then we largely forget this. This is part of Spirit's greater plan for us.

Even though we forget, there are ways to recall what we came here to do. Some people use meditation and spiritual practice to access the ***Akashic Records***, which are a sort of record hall that holds information about all our previous lifetimes, including what we learned, the people we interacted with, and what was left undone. Even without seeing these records, we can look to the events that take place in our lives, to the lessons that appear again and again for us, and get a sense of our greater purpose in this lifetime. Many people, myself included, are dedicated to this study.

As I have seen hundreds of times with my students and peers on the spiritual path, choosing to look at life this way brings a pivotal shift in our journey. It's a U-turn, the ultimate bend in the road. It's when, after traveling across mountains and plains for thousands of miles, we reach the shoreline and turn back again. When we embrace the events of this lifetime, good and bad, as part of our soul's story, we start to come home.

My student Lauren is a great example of this shift. She was born into a remarkably painful life, and as a child she experienced great trauma. When I met Lauren, she'd already spent years in therapy looking at the people and events that caused such strife in her early years. As many people do, she got to a point in her work where therapy alone wasn't enough. She turned to spirituality for the next phase of her healing. (Note that this also works in the opposite way; plenty of spiritually minded people eventually find that they need therapy and/or psychological techniques like those discussed in chapter 5 to move forward.)

Once Lauren started working in the spiritual realm, she really accepted for the first time that she is more than her trauma. She stepped into her power by starting to look at why her soul may have chosen the lessons it did and why it had received them in such a harsh way. This is when Lauren took on her role as a healer. She started with earth healing, working with animal Guides like the eagle and the white wolf. This helped her reclaim a sense of safety and grounding she had never felt before in this lifetime. Through that, she began working with her ancestors, communicating with them and helping them heal through her. She learned to cut cords, seeking out the old energies carried within her family line and releasing them. Then her Guides brought her into these deeper meditations where she would go on astral journeys to view her own soul story.

Today, Lauren leads others in this work. She is known as the Shadow Alchemist. By being vulnerable and open about her own past and the work she's done to heal it, she invites others to open up about their wounds with intention to learn from them. Her Guides led the entire process; Lauren's work was to become increasingly sensitive to their instruction. She started to follow the breadcrumbs of spiritual insight, and this is where they led her. She said yes to the lessons of this lifetime, as painful as they have been, and reconnected past, present, and future on the soul level.

When we embrace our life in this way, we find the road continues on and on.

My friend and colleague, author and professional psychic Lisa Campion, offered me a soul reading that ended up giving me greater insight into my concerns with scarcity and insecurity. About a week before the reading, I had a dream about my friend and fellow psychic, Diana.

In the dream, Diana and I were in a dark medieval-looking room. The walls were stone; the windows were covered in a heavy red velvet; and there was mahogany furniture all around. It felt like we were in a time very long ago, and I was aware that this was the home of a very wealthy person. The energy was heavy and thick there.

I sensed Diana's presence but was lucid enough to know she was no longer alive and I was dreaming, so I teased her, "Don't you dare show up in full apparition!" She laughed back and agreed to just accompany me in her energetic form. I slowly backed out of the room and into a hallway, playfully keeping my eye on her. Then I heard something behind me and whipped around.

There I saw a man with slight build and a very thin mustache. We made eye contact and he immediately swung his arm to attack me, hitting me in the back of my lower ribs on the right side. "No!" I shouted out in terror. Then I woke up.

When Lisa looked into my soul's story a few days later, she told me of a particular past life from hundreds of years ago. In it, I was a man who profited from war. "It was blood money," Lisa explained. She described that I had a brother who tried to help me get out of it, and that I spent much of that life trying to clean the blood from my hands through generosity, giving to charities and beggars. Yet I was not able to wipe it away completely, and I still carry some guilt and shame around money.

Lisa offered a meditation for me through which I could cleanse my relationship with money. She also suggested I would have to work on where I hold that experience in my body and pointed to the exact spot where I had been attacked in the dream.

Of course, I freaked out. "Lisa, how could you know?" I exclaimed. Yes, even psychics are still amazed by this stuff; the Universe is incredibly clever and it loves to show off.

That night I went into the meditation that Lisa had suggested. It was a visualization around washing the blood off money. I called in my Guides, expecting them to show me a little blood on some coins to wash off. Using my imagination, I visualized a small pile of gold with my third eye.

My Guides must have been laughing at that, because they doubled it, then doubled it again. In my mind's eye I saw the pile grow until it was a mountain of gold. And it was dripping, positively dripping, with blood. I was up to my elbows in it. I had no idea how I could possibly clean it all.

Yet when I asked my Guides for help, they just started hosing the blood off. At first it dripped down bright red, but as it was doused in water, it became pink, then pale pink, then clear. I looked down and saw that my hands were clean. The next thing I knew, I saw the little man from my dream standing in front of me, smiling. He was so happy. He introduced himself as my brother from that lifetime and told me he was proud of me for finally doing the work. Then he promised that I would move into a space of abundance again and wouldn't need to worry so much about making things happen. Through this interaction, I was no longer afraid of him—or of money. I understood why I'd struggled so much with insecurity in this lifetime. Beyond just the childhood I experienced this time around, I was able to see how it connected to my soul's story.

Near the end of the meditation my Guides showed me an image of the house I'd sold. I looked at it fondly, then realized something was wrong. It was sort of pixelated, made up of tiny circles that began to shine in the light.

Suddenly there was a *POP!* and the circles began to fall to the floor. They were gold coins! I knew this image was a gift to me, a sort of cord-cutting with the house itself. Now, every time I think about having left the house, I see it crumbling to the ground, the sound of clinking metal all around me.

This work is never over. We will be students until the day we die—you, me, and everyone else.

It helps a lot to do this work throughout our life. But if we're destined to do it, we can also get a whole lot done right at the end. Remember, all of us undergo life review in the period following our death. This gives us greater context for the lessons we've learned in this lifetime and where they come from—it's like the work Lauren does or the reading Lisa led me through. Many of us will also experience a good deal of this in the days, weeks, and even months prior to our death.

My friend Tom provides a good example here. He passed away last year. Tom definitely didn't want to die, but when his cancer treatments stopped working, he understood where he was headed and leaned into it. He wasn't a very spiritual person prior to that, but he did a 180 as his health declined and started asking me about my work, meeting with healers and a priest, and doing a preemptive life review to make sense of it all. He wasn't frantic, though he was highly motivated. The priest he was meeting with told his wife, "I have never seen anybody more at peace in leaving this space than Tom." Watching Tom face death was a validating and powerful experience for me. It was a reminder that we can engage with what life is all about at any moment, if we choose.

That's what our Guides want for us: they want us to decide to meet our lives, with all their challenges and lessons, exactly where they are. And we don't need to wait until we're dying—and certainly not until we have died—to do it. Showing up for our lives in this way offers us a glimpse of our soul's greater story. This is the ultimate antidote to impatience. Suddenly we have space to consider that maybe we haven't manifested what we want because something better is coming or maybe things are falling apart because it's time for us to become a new Madonna. Even when challenges are falling in our way one after another like a row of dominoes, we can wonder what we're meant to learn from that: whether we came for a difficult life in general, whether we chose to pack our troubles into a shorter span of time to get them over with, or whether our life is trying to show us we can approach our challenges in a new way.

When we make the shift into seeing our soul's story, we're transported right smack-dab into the now. We can recognize that not only are we not there yet, but we're never going to get there—and that's OK. In fact, it's the best news of all.

EXERCISE: HONOR THE PAUSE

It's time for a DIY exercise! That means you can choose to do this in the way that works best for you.

As I've seen in my students, it can be a little unsettling to choose your own adventure. I really believe you can do this! Ask your Guides to show you which version of this exercise will work best for you, and then trust the very first answer you receive. I often prefer to see myself going into my spiritual temple and asking my Guides to arrive and talk to me. This helps me really get into the zone. Others like to access this state while performing a monotonous task or running. You may prefer visualization, automatic writing, walking, channeling aloud—whatever calls you. These are your Guides, and this is your practice.

Whichever practice you choose, enter into it with cleansing and grounding. Then call in your Guides.

Choose to focus on something that's bringing up impatience for you in this phase of your life. Allow yourself to feel how it is to not have a resolution or not to have manifested what you'd hoped to have manifested by now or to have a vague sense of being "late" or "behind." Then ask your Guides: "What is the purpose of this pause? Why do things feel so slow? What does this have to show me?"

The pause itself has power. Everything is divinely orchestrated, even this! Allow your Guides to tell or show you the answers you seek.

They may show you any number of things, but there are some common possibilities. Maybe something better is coming your way. Maybe you're being protected. Maybe there's something for you to learn while you wait that is going to serve you in a critical moment in the future. Maybe you need a shift in perspective. Maybe someone else is being served by this pause, and your soul has committed to helping them. Be curious and you may find an answer that surprises you!

Once you receive the guidance you need, offer gratitude. You may want to say aloud what you're grateful for or write it down in a gratitude journal or feed your gratitude jar. Thank your Guides for sharing what they have shared and for everything they chose not to share, too. Know that things are the way they are for a reason. Thank your Guides and yourself, and take the answer you received with you going forward. It may help you be more patient or, at the very least, to be patient with your own impatience!

Chapter 7

GO LEFT—NO, RIGHT—NO, LEFT!

WE'VE ALL BEEN THERE: WE'RE CRUISING ALONG WITHOUT A care in the world when we come to an intersection. The GPS tells us to go one way, the paper map another, and then someone in the back seat pipes up to say, "Well, you can also go straight..." We sit there, riddled with confusion, unsure of where to turn. Our minds become scrambled, and we can react in ways that don't make much sense.

Receiving directions that are confusing, conflicting, or even contradictory is a common problem. It's annoying at best and paralyzing at worst. It seems to have little to do with how far along we are in the process, because this is something that comes up even for my most advanced students—as well as me! It helps immensely to realize that no matter which way we turn, Spirit can always keep guiding us in the direction of our evolution. Even if we ignore them time and again, our Guides will continue to offer us assistance. They will never turn their back on us or leave us alone.

Still, it can be hard to make sense of what our Guides are saying when other voices of fear or shame get in the way. Many of us are still haunted by past experiences. It takes work to keep our eyes on the road and move forward. The more we spin out in our heads, the more difficult this becomes, so staying grounded in the present moment is of the utmost importance.

It can also help to give our Guides a way to work with us directly, bypassing our mental chatter with something concrete. Tarot cards, angel cards, or, my personal favorite, oracle cards, can clear away the clutter in our minds and bring some focus. We can also ask for a sign, as you may have noticed I do often. As always, we want to work from and for the greatest and highest good and seek out the most positive interpretation for the message we receive.

This chapter is all about what happens when we get confused. To start, let's consider one of the biggest concerns many of us have: the fear of making a wrong decision.

Wrong Turns

Fear is one of the ego's greatest tricks. It tells us there's something wrong with us. It suggests that deep down, we don't know what's best. It picks apart our past decisions and keeps us from making new ones, instilling in us the anxiety that we will choose incorrectly and suffer as a result.

As with so many things, for me this comes down to perspective. When we look at life as a winding road full of adventure, we can't choose wrong; we can only make a choice that leaves the road a little longer. And on a road trip, a little longer isn't a bad thing. We never know what amazing park or highway is just off the main route, waiting for us to discover it. Some of the best things can come to us from so-called "wrong" turns, which become side routes when we continue to follow our guidance.

Mel is the daughter of a dear friend of mine. She'd grown up on Long Island and had always dreamed of moving to California. Her two best friends did, too, and the three girls planned to go together after high school. Instead of going to college after graduation, Mel waited tables and managed to sock away savings every month, all with the goal of a city life in mind. Her friends, however, ended up making different plans: one moved in with a boyfriend, and another went to college out of state. Mel didn't want to give up, though; nothing was stopping her from achieving her dream. When she was twenty years old, she finally felt ready to make it happen, so she packed her little car and bravely drove West—even though she didn't know anyone out there. She sublet a room for a few months to start, intending to sign a lease once she had a steady job.

The room was small and the roommates weren't friendly, so Mel ended up spending a lot of time—and money—exploring LA. Her bank account dwindled far more quickly than she'd expected. She applied for positions at all sorts of restaurants, but she couldn't manage to get even a single interview. The few dates she went on were all duds, and her attempts at making new friends left her even lonelier than before. By the time the sublet ended, she couldn't wait to leave.

Mel was both broke and defeated when she turned around and drove all the way back home to her parents' house. It really felt like she'd made a wrong decision because nothing had worked out for her. Just a few months in California and not only was that dream dead, but so was her motivation for doing anything else.

I saw Mel when my husband and I went to her parents' house for dinner, and we had a little chat together on the porch swing while the others were inside. "I just feel so stupid for having pushed to move anyway, even though I was doing it alone. I should have listened. On some level, I knew it wasn't going to work," Mel said with resignation.

Her experience resonated with me. How often have I pushed to manifest something that I knew just wasn't quite right? "It can be really hard to know the difference between something that's just challenging and something that's misaligned," I said. "I don't think you should consider this as a misstep. If you hadn't gone, it would have been a dream unfulfilled."

"More like a nightmare," Mel said.

"Maybe so," I answered, as I felt the channel to my own Guides open and allowed them to speak. "But you learned from it. You're back here making a new dream. And now you get to ask yourself: what's that new dream going to look like?"

A few months later, Mel's mother told me she had enrolled at the local community college. She enjoyed being a student and working toward a degree. She met another young woman through her classes, and a few years later they ended up moving together to the San Francisco Bay Area. This time, Mel had the education and experience to get an administrative job at a law office. Her friend and roommate was a companion for her, and together they went out and met lots of new people. Just a few years after her initial attempt to move to California, Mel was loving living on the bay.

I was pleased to hear that Mel hadn't given up. She hadn't become jaded or refused to go back to California when the time was right. Instead, she had learned from her short experience what she needed to make the move more successful. By the time she was ready to put her plan into action, California was ready for her. This simply couldn't have happened without her earlier experience in Los Angeles, as heartbreaking as it had been for her.

She also learned how to listen to the voice she described to me on the porch swing: the part of her that knew it wasn't going to work. It can be really difficult to decipher the difference between that voice of guidance and regular old fear. (I've got more on that to come; read on.) Mel's experience highlights an important point: with almost every perceived "wrong" turn, there is some sort of guidance we're ignoring. When we live and learn from our experience, we get better at discerning which voices are worth our attention.

That's why none of these turns are actually *wrong*—they're instructive. They're part of the route we're building for ourselves, even if it isn't the most direct line from point A to point B. This can seem counterintuitive in a society that is all about immediate gratification, but our Guides are always leading us to find value in these little side trips without worrying too much about whether we're getting somewhere.

These deviations from the direct path often serve us in some indirect way as well. We may meet someone, come across an idea, or learn something entirely new to us. That job we took only to quit a month later may have introduced us to the friend who later got us a new job; that overseas vacation that felt like a total bust may have inspired us to get to know our local area better.

And at the very least, when we take what feels like a wrong turn, we eliminate options. If Mel had not met a new friend who wanted to move to California with her and if her own dream of moving West had truly died when her initial trip out there went awry, she could have chosen to see it as freeing, knowing she would never have to wonder what moving to the city might have gotten her. It's OK to experience things and realize they didn't work and we don't want to do them again. That's a perfectly reasonable response to have—and one that is valuable enough to justify having made the decision in the first place. Sometimes we just need to learn exactly what we do or don't want, and that isn't a waste of time. It's actually really productive.

I want to be clear that this is totally optional. If you want to look at your life as a series of mistakes, you can absolutely use your free will to do so. Working with that pattern may even be part of your soul's contract—a preincarnation spiritual agreement outlining the lessons and relationships a soul will encounter to support growth, balance and evolution.

But there's an entirely different option available—one our Guides are hoping we'll eventually adopt: a way of seeing our world as an inherently positive place, where everything we do leads us closer to our soul's destination. I don't want to skim over the surface here; I'm not suggesting that things like disappointment and heartbreak and regret aren't real or that they should be smashed down and not felt. But when we feel them without attaching too much of our identity to them, we find more positive emotional truths are available for us. We begin to enjoy the twists and turns without wishing we were going in a straight line. And when this happens—when we refuse to accept the very idea of a wrong turn—a whole new reality opens up. This is when our Guides start to cheer, because now they can get down to work.

Though I encourage you to see the world as devoid of wrong turns, it's important to note that we can definitely run ourselves in circles so much that we don't get anywhere. This happens when we ignore our intuitive GPS entirely or even turn it off. Even this isn't a wrong turn, though—as long as we take action to get out of it.

Getting Lost

When we ignore the guidance available to us again and again, we can get into a dangerous situation. We aren't permanently lost in the sense of not having a way back—it's always possible to make a U-turn or find a new route with the help of our Guides. But in the short term we can lose ourselves or our highest knowing for a time. In our worst moments, we all have the capacity to stray from our highest and greatest good. This is always harmful to us, and sometimes even harmful to others. In the worst cases it can last a very long time.

I am acquainted with someone I will call Franklin, who has struggled for decades with alcoholism. Though he's at the point where he's aware he's an alcoholic, Franklin seems unwilling to do anything about it. He wants to believe it's everybody else's fault but his own. Addiction controls him so that he can't see things clearly, let alone hear his guidance. My heart breaks for him because I know it's truly a disease. He has lost friends, family, a marriage, kids . . . the list goes on. It would take enormous effort for him to really stand up to his alcoholism, and after that point, it will take a long-term commitment and probably plenty of false starts before he's able to heal. But it is possible. Until he is able to put in the work, though, he will remain lost.

This is a heartbreaking reality to witness—and I suspect an even more heartbreaking one to experience. Though addiction has not been part of my story this lifetime, I know the kind of head trip that can come with realizing I've been avoiding what my Guides have to say. My experience on Cora Street marked one of the lower points in my life. Had I let them, the challenges I faced there could have been all-consuming. Between the bad boyfriend I had as a young teen and the man I lived with on Cora Street in my early twenties, I was teetering on the edge of a cycle of abusive relationships. (I was fortunate to have a really wonderful boyfriend between these two who deserves credit! I mention these difficult relationships to show how self-destructive situations often have a hold over us, if that's part of our soul's contract, and they can repeat as their own sort of addiction.) Luckily, I was able to shift the pattern. Though the relationship I got into after I left Cora Street ultimately ended in divorce, it was largely a healthy one, and I followed it with the beautiful one I share with my husband today.

So what is it that allows us to drive in a few circles without fully getting lost?

First, reaching out to our Guides often and at least listening to what they have to say can put a limit on this holding pattern. Even if you aren't willing to follow the directions you're given, keep the volume on your GPS turned up. This is key.

Second, stay in the present moment. It can be easy to just focus on our past decisions and everything that didn't go as we'd hoped. In chapter 5, we looked at how valuable it can be to reconsider our past by answering the question, *When did this start?* There is a big difference between engaging the past intentionally like that and spending our whole lives there rethinking everything that did or didn't happen. We have to accept that what's happened has happened; it cannot be changed.

Aimee is a friend of mine who is perpetually living in chaos. She makes major life changes at least once a year—a new job, a new home—and is chronically unstable as a result. She lives at the edge of her means and often slightly above it, which keeps her in long-term debt and limits her choices going forward. Though that kind of instability would, of course, drive me absolutely nuts, it isn't inherently bad—except that Aimee herself is quite unhappy with it.

In our conversations, I've heard Aimee refer again and again to the people who, as she sees it, put her in this situation. She frequently refers to having bad luck with employment, speaking about this or that bad boss or colleagues who had it out for her. The homes she lives in always seem to have bad neighbors, bad landlords, or both. She often says things like, "This person made me lose my job," or "I would have kept living there, but I couldn't be next door to him anymore." There is such a thing as bad luck, and while I have compassion for that, I am doubtful that it can play such a role in Aimee's life because I also see her making a whole lot of choices that don't get her where she says she wants to go. The attention she pays to everyone who has wronged her seems unreasonable: Aimee will often talk about things that happened five or even ten years ago, explaining where she might be today if things had gone differently.

Yet Aimee doesn't want to take steps toward change herself. She's hoping it will come in from the outside—that someone or something might arrive to save her. She goes from psychic to psychic, asking what she needs to do. The answers she receives, not only from myself but from other psychics, to stay put, take concrete actions that will help stabilize her life, and look for the underlying cause of her discontent don't land within her, so she simply asks the same questions again. Ironically, she has spent a lot of money doing this. I had to decide to stop reading for her because it feels more destructive than helpful.

From what I can tell from the outside, Aimee's attraction to chaos is part of her soul contract. She was bound to struggle with instability somehow in her life. But there are also things she could do about that. There's something for her to learn if she can go back, figure out where her affinity for instability started this time around, and make peace with the fact that this is not just a series of events that have happened *to* her but a give-and-take relationship between herself and her life. Her Guides can show her how to get out of this cycle, but until she activates her free will, things will remain the same. This whole process starts with letting go of what has already taken place and moving forward.

One key piece for Aimee to recognize is that there is no other version of reality where things went differently than they did. In chapter 3, I explained the possibilities present when we jump timelines. This should not be taken to mean we can alter the course of time itself. We can always make choices that affect things going forward, but we cannot go back. Imagining what might have been is an enormous energy suck that brings nothing useful into our lives. It is its own form of addiction and leaves us lost, driving in circles instead of moving on with our lives.

Once she can get past this rumination, I suspect Aimee's Guides might lead her to choose something difficult. They might ask her to stick out a job with someone she doesn't get along with, even if it's by finding a way to befriend that person. Or they might ask her to live well below her means for a time while she pays off debt or move to a lower cost of living area, finding ways to brighten this experience by making her home her sanctuary or listening to spiritual podcasts on her commute. I don't want to pretend I have Aimee's solution—that's between her and her Guides. What I do have is a sense of how they might ask her to make a change: slowly, one step at a time. This can be hard to accept. We often think our Guides will wave a wand and make things easy or immediate, but that isn't necessarily the case. Often the most spiritual solution is the one that requires significant real-world effort. Whatever their advice, I know Aimee's Guides are ready to lead her out of the circles she is repeating in life. And that starts with her being fed up enough with that circling to be willing to be done with it once and for all.

Getting lost is an unfortunate reality for many of us. Yet as so many have experienced, all it takes is a single choice to break the cycle and set us free. Our Guides are always there, waiting to illuminate that choice for us. Seeing it as a single choice doesn't mean it's a single step—it can take work to reset ourselves after years of destructive behavior. Still it will all come down to the moment we really, truly say to ourselves, *I'm done with this*, and finish that part of our soul's contract.

The choice between staying lost and moving forward, for most of us, is clear. Our Guides can always point us in the right direction to make this possible. But what do we do when we know exactly where we are, yet we find ourselves spinning over and over about where that is?

Spinning in 360s

Though 360s are technically circles, they don't get us lost—they spin us right off the road. The directions are clear; we know where we're headed; but suddenly we start spiraling in our heads, going over and over "the meaning of it all."

Throughout this book, I've encouraged you to contextualize your experiences and make sense of what's happening in your life following the guidance that's available to you. Yet it's time to acknowledge that there's a danger in overdoing this, in getting so up in our heads that we can't move forward.

I recently mentored a woman, Suze, who has a tendency to do this. It was Suze's third mentorship session with me, and we talked about the same thing we did during the other two sessions, which is how Suze got divorced around the same time I did and has not connected with anyone else romantically since then. Though she yearns for another relationship, she overthinks her every interaction with potential partners, becoming clingy after a single date. In short, though she takes responsibility for her role in ending the marriage, it doesn't lead her to do anything productive. Instead, she is locked up in regret and self-doubt, wondering what she could do differently in a next time that never comes.

In my workshops and mentorship sessions over the years, I've seen this type of thing show up a lot. I think it may be more common among people on a spiritual path. It's a confused interpretation of the meaning of this work: yes, we should work on ourselves, but we are entirely misunderstanding things if we take that to mean we are broken and need to be fixed.

Our Guides are here to teach us, but that isn't a punishment—it's a privilege. Being alive and having things to learn is a gift. This lifetime, however challenging it may be, is an opportunity to experience joy. Our spirituality is supposed to give us energy, not drain it away, and if we find ourselves chronically depleted by the process, it indicates something is very wrong.

When we find ourselves spinning in 360s, the most useful thing we can do is look for the humor in the situation. I'm not talking about sinking deep into self-deprecating humor (though a little bit is OK); I'm talking about finding the joy and levity we had when we chose this lifetime, with all the lessons it brings to us.

This is especially important as we deepen the work on ourselves, looking for when we developed our habits or waiting for a specific contract to be completed. I've had to utilize humor a whole lot to deal with the feelings of inadequacy and low self-worth that have come up during menopause, seeking out reasons to laugh and be light. And in my housing process, I've had to frequently find lightness in the fact that, though the situation is very difficult for me, it's not that difficult from the outside. "Are you even serious?" I exclaim in faux shock as I explain to my friends about the newest symptom of my hormone shift. "Work on this *again*?!" I laugh as I encounter some new aspect of my insecurity raising its ugly head.

Humor offers us a lighter way to take accountability for the situation—one that still owns that it is uniquely ours while poking fun at our own resistance to that responsibility. It makes space for us to find joy, even in our suffering. We don't have to take everything so seriously, as it turns out; sometimes, even when we're flying completely out of control, we can still enjoy the view. After all, this is supposed to be fun.

And the truth is, no matter how much work we do, there are going to be aspects of this lifetime we will never understand. We can ascribe meaning to events in our lives to the point that it's helpful, but we can also put that work down at any moment if it isn't. It simply isn't worth the effort to torture ourselves by making too much meaning out of small events; we're much better served when we approach our lives in a balanced way. There are some bad days that don't have reasons and some tragedies that will never make sense. That's OK. It doesn't mean we're doing something wrong or giving up. The deeper we get into this work with our Guides, the easier it is to discern the difference.

If you suspect you may be falling into the trap of overthinking, it can be helpful to ask your Guides questions: Have I done my work here? Am I doing enough? What do I have to learn? Every once in a while the answer you'll hear back is something to the effect of *Yes. Stop. Rest. Give it a break.* Or, *Laugh. Enjoy other aspects of your life. Isn't this ridiculous?* If the answer feels intuitively right, it probably is.

Our Guides are always leading us toward the lesson. Yet sometimes we struggle to understand what exactly they are saying—especially when the voice of fear is involved. How do we cut through the mental chatter and identify which voices are ours and which ones we are receiving from Spirit?

Deciphering Mixed Messages

In moments of stress, it can be really hard to distinguish between the voice of our own thoughts and the voice of our Guides. This is even truer when fear gets involved in a situation, because fear is often really persistent in its delivery. While I've gotten much better at telling the difference between the two, I still have plenty of opportunities to practice.

Several years ago, a friend and I drove into Manhattan for an event. We ran into traffic along the way and were feeling rushed, so we picked a parking garage quickly, left the car, and hurried to the venue. The next few hours were a blur—we had a great time, talked to lots of people, and by the time the event was over we were exhausted but happy. As we walked outside, she said, "Where are we parked again?"

Where, indeed. I had no idea. A quick online search showed numerous parking garages in the immediate vicinity, each of them surely containing multiple levels filled with row after row of cars. Somewhere in the back of my mind I remembered a sign saying that the garage closed at midnight. I checked my phone again: it was 11:40 p.m.

I felt a tightness in my gut as my mind started to whir. Looking back, this was one of the first instances of the hormonally driven anxiety I would later treat as a symptom of menopause; at the time, though, all I knew was that it felt like I was listening to a thousand voices at once, each of them elucidating their own creative doomsday scenario. I took a deep breath and asked for the voice of the highest and greatest good to come through.

You're going to find your car. It was immediate.

Shortly after, fear stepped in again, and I heard all the worst cases that could possibly arise. Maybe we would never find it; maybe we would have to get a cab all the way back to Long Island; maybe there would be no cabs and no hotels and we'd end up sleeping on the street. Maybe this, maybe that, maybe something else, maybe, maybe, maybe . . . I breathed again, focusing on the highest and greatest good.

You're going to find your car. My belly settled, and I relaxed.

As we set off to find it, I stayed focused on this voice, clearing my head every time it got loud in there by asking for the highest and greatest good to come through. It wasn't easy, but it gave my Guides space to work. Fifteen minutes later we were in the car and headed home.

The truth is that there really are no mixed messages; Spirit's voice is one and the same. Our Guides don't argue or even disagree with each other. But fear and its henchmen—worry, doubt, shame, uncertainty, and the like—can sound a lot like guidance and can mess with our head pretty easily. Ego can do the same thing, sneaking in through comparison or expectation.

Asking to receive guidance from the highest and greatest good cuts through this right away. What we find is that the answers we receive are short and sweet. They get straight to the point without elaborating. This distinguishes them immediately from fear and ego, which tend to go on and on, offering a variety of scenarios that *might* come to pass. True guidance isn't about what happened or what will happen, but rather about this exact moment. When we follow that guidance, we start living right here, right now—which is the only place that actually matters.

Requesting an answer from the highest and greatest good connects us with our own accountability and willingness to do the work. We are always accountable for the actions we take based on the messages we receive, in part because we are the ones responsible for how we interpret those messages. Our minds want to make much more out of the intuitive input we receive than is actually there; they have a tendency to scramble the message, adding details or putting a spin on things based on our emotional experience. This isn't a design flaw: we're meant to expand the energy around the message our Guides send us and co-create with it. When we call for the highest and greatest good, not only do we cut through the noise, we remind ourselves that our own interpretation should come from this place as well. Our contribution should come from the very best part of us—the part that knows and trusts that the Universe is an inherently good place and that everything we experience in life is here to teach us something.

This is the responsibility that breaks us free from any tendency to get lost in self-destruction or spin out in our heads. The highest and greatest good in the Universe is also within each of us; it's what unites us with the spiritual realm, bringing heaven down to earth.

In the moments we really struggle to access the highest and greatest good, tools can really help. I'm a particular fan of using cards and keep oracle decks from luminaries such as Kyle Gray, Colette Baron-Reid, Meggan Watterson, and Gabrielle Bernstein in several rooms of my house for intuitive emergencies or just general mood pick-me-ups. I ask my Guides to point me toward the deck I need in the moment, and then I get to work. Usually bearing both an image and a mantra, cards help us focus on just a couple of things at once—a real achievement when our minds are busy! The very best decks lead us toward concrete action we can take in our lives.

The following scenario has happened to me many times: I have decisions to make, and instead of leaning into my guidance, I start stressing in my head. This compounds, as the chattier my mind becomes, the less I'm able to hear my Guides. (Sound familiar yet?) This whole process starts to exhaust me, leaving me with less and less energy to address the situation, and I find myself calling out to my Guides in annoyance, almost as if I'm reprimanding them: "Where are you? Can you give me *something* to work with?"

Sometimes I actually hear the answer, and other times I intuit it: *Go pull a card.* My seeing the image and the words helps my Guides get through to me, even when my head is busy.

To work with decks, it helps to know what and how to ask. We're best served when we focus on open-ended questions with direction attached to them. I suggest questions that start with *Show me*, *Lead me*, or *Offer me*, or questions that set up a conversation. Don't shy away from your own responsibility in a given situation; "Show me what I need to know" is much more useful than "Show me what will happen next March 7 at 6:38 p.m.," because your Guides' job isn't to save you; it's to lead you to the answer within yourself. When we ask from a place of the highest and greatest good, yearning to connect with our inner knowledge through honest curiosity, we find that these answers are always there.

Whether the messages we received were what confused us or our confusion was simply one of the things we came here to face and overcome, we can always shift things back toward clarity and keep going. In some cases, that adjustment is simple; in others, it takes more time. But once we manage to make a change, we find ourselves cruising along again as if nothing has happened. When you reach this point, remember to look out at the scenery and open the windows to feel the air on your face. The whole Universe was waiting for you to come on back, and it's ready to lend a hand to keep you cruising along.

EXERCISE: WORKING WITH DECKS

If you're hearing information that's confusing, contradictory, or even conflicting or if your mind is just interjecting itself into the process in a way that isn't welcome, cards are a great way to set it all straight. This exercise can be used with just about any randomized card deck such as oracle, affirmation, angel, or Spirit Guide cards—including my *The Guide(s) Deck*!

If you're clear enough to remember, cleanse and ground yourself—or just take a breath and ask that it will be done. You can ask for guidance on which deck to use if you have multiple (and you can also ask your Guides which one will help you most if you're purchasing a deck for the first time!). Then pick up your deck and sit with your quandary for a moment. Really allow yourself to feel the emotions that come with your situation—what is it you need to know, and how do you want to feel once you know it?

Next it's time to pick a card. Shuffle the deck a little bit to mix the cards. Then find your question.

It's important to frame the question in a way that is open-ended and allows our Guides to lead us to our highest knowing. Questions that ask when or for a yes or no are not useful in this process, so opt for something like "Show me what can help me," "What is it I need to know?" or "How can I know whom to ask?" Our Guides love to teach us experientially, so the best questions lead us to a real-world action that we have to take.

Once you've found your question, ask it from a space of true curiosity, connecting with the highest and greatest good. Then, allow your inner knowing to draw you to the right card. Don't overthink it, and don't dismiss any small *this one!* or *that one!* that comes up from the depths of your being. Remember: true guidance will be short and sweet. If you get a whole lot of explanation (*this one, because it's blue and blue means…*), it's probably your mind. Also be sure to notice any signs that may take place while you're choosing—these are there to help you know which card is yours. Many times, your card will even drop or fly out of the deck on its own!

When you've found your card, take a few minutes to study it. Allow it to bring up any associations for you and trust them when they arrive—remember, psychic information comes in through our own frame of reference, so don't dismiss your own imagination or memory. What is this card trying to show you? What does it mean for your life? What is it asking you to do, see, believe, think, or say? Your Guides will always lead you toward accountability and real-world action.

In the rare case that you really can't make sense of the message you've received, you can ask for a second card for clarification.

When you're finished with the deck, offer it gratitude and put it away. You can leave the card you chose out for up to a day to remind you of the message from your Guides, but remember to put it away respectfully in a timely manner. After you're finished with the deck, be sure to seal the practice somehow by meditating, automatic writing, journaling, or taking a contemplative walk. May this entire process bring you the clarity you're seeking!

Chapter 8

TRAFFIC JAMS, DETOURS, AND PIT STOPS

AS WE WIND DOWN THE ROAD, WE'RE JUST ABOUT GUARANTEED to experience a few holdups along the way. While it's impossible to foresee the exact *when* and *how* we will run into these things, we can be sure that they will show up at some point.

We've all had this one happen: we're cruising at a steady pace when suddenly we see brake lights. We slow down, then slow more, and eventually find ourselves at an absolute standstill. In life, this happens when something obstructs our path—and as often as not, *we are* that something. It's easy to get into panic paralysis, in which we feel like nothing is going right and, in our anxiety about it, accidentally start manifesting worse and worse things. We enter a negative pattern we can't escape.

Luckily for us, our Guides are well-versed at handling this situation. All we need to do is call out to them, and they will send help. Sometimes this comes in the form of a detour that gets us out of the jam we are in. They can send us a set of actions to take or, even more often, a new perspective to adopt, showing us how we can look at our situation differently and set ourselves free. We often find that the detour our Guides offer is a better path than the one we had before. Other times, our Guides will send us a pit crew to spiff us up and get us back on the road. This pit crew can bring that new perspective, helping us avoid a breakdown in the long run and make the best use of our time while we're feeling stuck.

Whatever they send, it's best to offer our Guides gratitude for their help. This, too, brings a pivotal perspective shift that can ensure once we're going again, we keep powering forward without obstruction.

This chapter is all about handling life's jams. If—or better yet, when—you're feeling stuck, consider how your Guides can help! They may just surprise you with their creativity and willingness to step in.

Roadblock!

No matter what is blocking the road ahead, it's up to you to figure out what you're going to do about it.

I recently had a session with a mentee who is in a really difficult professional situation. Cassie works for a big and well-known international hotel company with dozens of locations around the world. She is young, and her parents run a corporate travel agency, which has given them some connections in the tourism industry. She declined her parents' offer of help finding a job when she got out of college and was thrilled to land an entry-level role at a respectable company in a city she loved all on her own.

The problem was that the hotel manager was a total jerk, just an incredibly negative and challenging person. Cassie quickly came to understand that the reason the job was open in the first place was that no one really liked to work at this location. Cassie was regularly degraded and condescended to, and though the manager treated the whole staff like scum, he was quick to take credit for the high ratings customers gave them for their service. Cassie explained to me how she'd been ready to quit when she was fortuitously offered a promotion if she moved to another city. Excited to explore a new place, she quickly accepted the transfer and moved.

But the dream turned into a nightmare in no time. The manager at the new hotel was even worse. Cassie heard her call other employees mean nicknames, and on her third day of work, she had suggested that Cassie was stupid. "I didn't even think it was possible for things to get worse!" Cassie said, "I'm fine financially. I love my new apartment. I joined a gym and a painting class and am making new friends. I spend every waking hour exploring new restaurants and bars on the weekends . . . But I *hate* having to work for this woman! How could this company keep employing people who are so toxic?"

Bullies, I heard Spirit say. ***Ask her more about bullies.***

So I asked Cassie about her relationship with bullying, and sure enough, she was quick to tell me she'd been picked on quite a bit throughout her life—by the other kids at school, by best frenemies over the years, and in several romantic relationships with people who turned out to be narcissists. She even told me how she had caught her ex-boyfriend in an affair with her own cousin. It seemed clear to me that Spirit was giving her an opportunity to turn that history of bullying around by speaking up for herself.

I felt the call to channel, so I asked Cassie if I could open for her Guides to speak through me and she agreed. They started suggesting ways for Cassie to empower herself at work, such as encouraging the other employees to write down their experiences and letting human resources know about the abusive environment at this branch of the hotel. Then I asked Cassie what she felt she was being guided to do. That's when she said, "Well, my dad keeps telling me he has an in at a boutique hotel in town who could get me started there, but I feel bad taking it. I don't want to be a nepo baby."

"You feel bad taking it," I repeated slowly so Cassie could hear her own words. "Let me get this straight. The Universe is giving you an out, and you're still saying no because you feel like you're taking advantage of your situation." Cassie nodded as I made space for Spirit to speak through my channel again. "They say, ***Don't you see how your perspective is flawed here?*** You're still viewing yourself as a victim, but what Spirit is trying to show you is that you have everything you need to get out of this situation and into something that's healthy for you." Spirit then peppered me with questions that I passed on to Cassie. "***When did you decide that you were worthy of this treatment?***" I asked. "***What's it going to take for you to insist that you're worthy of something better?***"

Through our conversation, Cassie began to see that her Guides were trying to show her it was time to step into her self-worth and develop boundaries around how she is treated. The painful situations in her life, both personal and professional, were leading her toward that. Cassie was able to tie it all back to experiences she had had as a young child on the playground when she was pushed around by some older kids who saw her as a target.

I told Cassie what I heard from her Guides: that while what was happening with her boss was terrible, her bigger problem was how she thinks about herself. "***Fix that, focus on that, and the rest will fall into line,***" I channeled, explaining that she'd still have to do things—either quit outright and move to the boutique hotel her father could arrange for her, file a complaint with human resources and stay on at her current job, or something else along those lines—but her Guides would lead her to know which of these options was best for her. "But only when you do the inner work," I repeated, "because until you do, what's happening on the outside is guaranteed to happen again."

When we're stuck in a pattern like that, personal responsibility is the thing that helps us break free. We go from seeing a sea of brake lights ahead to watching the path open for us. This happens when we really seek to understand it, working with our Guides to see *why* we are stuck and what we need to do differently to get out of the cycle.

It's critical to note that responsibility is different from blame. Cassie is not responsible for the pattern of bullying that is manifesting in her life. But she is responsible for continuing to put up with it instead of taking steps toward change. Her soul came here to learn about empowerment, and she was getting an incredible chance to do so through this situation.

Once we start taking those steps, the Universe often reroutes us. Our Guides will indicate a secret back road that gets us out of the jam. It's once again our responsibility to follow their directions, listening carefully and making quick moves to maneuver our way back to the flow.

Rerouting...

These secret back routes can show up in the most unlikely ways.

I'm grateful that the coronavirus pandemic did not harm my family in any major way. Like everyone, we were shocked by the events that took place in those early weeks. Living in the New York area, in such close proximity to one of the hot spots during the first wave of transmission, was tragic and scary (yes, even for a psychic!). As the world shut down into silence and distance, my family and I were as bewildered and unsettled as our neighbors. But none of my family members who contracted coronavirus ended up gravely ill or suffered from long-term effects. And though everyone experienced the fallout of the pandemic with some degree of challenge, everyone in my family was able to recover within a year or two.

I had been a practicing psychic medium for more than a decade when the events of 2020 rolled out. Yet I had just begun to see my career as a fully legitimate income source—as legitimate as my husband's successful career in construction. Just a few months before this, I had done a meditation led by the best-selling author and podcaster Jay Shetty wherein I envisioned myself as a breadwinner for the very first time. I'd stumbled upon a career in psychic mediumship, but I'd never seen myself as a provider. The meditation had introduced me to the idea that it was possible for my family to rely, at least in part, on my income, instead of seeing it as an extra fund to pay for vacations and fun stuff.

That was fortuitous, because the construction industry, like so many others, ground to a near standstill in the spring of 2020, putting many of my husband's projects on pause. Amazingly, it was at that exact same moment that my projects really took off. When social distancing measures first went into effect, I called for an emergency meeting with Stephen and Jane, who help me with many aspects of my business and keep me organized (thank goodness!). Initially, I held the meeting because I wanted to know how I could keep my obligations with the clients I already had scheduled. "I know it's possible to still serve," I said, certain that if I said it then it would be true.

Stephen and Jane asked me if I'd heard of Zoom. I hadn't. I'd held plenty of phone readings over the years and even a few over FaceTime, but the majority were still in person. This limited me to working with people who lived in my immediate vicinity. I moved the meetings I had already scheduled online, tentatively learning my way around the software.

As the week went on, I got more and more requests for readings. People found themselves suddenly unsure about the power structures they had come to rely on. Others were just bombarded with the psychic information floating around the atmosphere—fear, discomfort, reorganization, and the opportunity for quick evolution. So I continued to speak it into existence: "This is an opportunity for my work to go deeper," I'd say, repeating affirmations for myself. "I am a breadwinner. My work has real value. My family can count on me." Though I was confirming my manifestation many times a day, putting it on order from the Universe, I still had no idea that going online would expand my business the way it did.

I kept getting sign-ups for readings—but something else happened, too. In the long hours spent at home, many people had started wondering what they really wanted to be doing with their lives. The psychic atmosphere continued to spin with information, and those with strong intuitive gifts started hearing the call to develop their skills. ***Tell them what you know,*** my Guides encouraged, so I posted and shared online in an attempt to reach others in their time of need. This grew my social following significantly, which allowed me to tell even more people about what I do and how I do it. My community started asking for more than readings: they started asking for mentorship.

I began hosting online workshops. My first one went well, and several students wanted to continue. I developed another workshop to meet their needs, then another, until I had six levels of training to offer. In the process, I stepped into my role as a breadwinner.

Service is an amazing energy booster. Spirit loves it when we are in service. Our Guides are constantly trying to lead us there because it's where some of our best work happens. Not only did I serve more people, but I thrived while doing so. For years, I'd been hearing that it was time to back off of readings and up my mentoring game. Teaching comes naturally to me. Yet I don't know that I would have had the courage to make the shift had I not had hundreds of people suddenly requesting mentorship. These factors—along with a whole lot of luck—helped me experience the pandemic in a positive way, even amid the chaos. I truly acknowledged being a breadwinner for the first time in my life, which in turn allowed me to flourish. This attracted better and better energy to me and my work.

For me, being a breadwinner is about so much more than money. It's about shifting from seeing myself as someone who is *taken care of* by others to seeing myself as someone who is a *productive provider* for my family. It's something I hadn't envisioned for myself since my kids were born, when I got out of my retail career to be a stay-at-home mom—a move that was appropriate for that moment in my life but not forever. With my kids in college, it was time to revisit my image of myself. And when I did, I found that I was able to run a successful business based on my talents, which is a huge self-esteem booster. In that way, the pandemic forced a detour—one I likely never would have chosen, but that led me where I needed to go.

This is precisely the type of detour our Guides can show us. A detour is a quick pivot, a turn we didn't expect, and we often don't have any idea where it's going. When we take one turn after another, listening to the guidance that's available to us, we find a path we may never have imagined. It brings us where we were always going anyway, but in a quicker, more effective, and often more pleasant way than if we'd stayed on the main road.

Our lives show us when a detour is necessary. Our circumstances shift and suddenly, though we had just been cruising without problems, we've ground to a halt. This is the moment to look around and see what other options are available. Those other options are our Guides showing us which way to go.

Just this week I spoke with a woman who is trying to get back to her spiritual practice now that she's a mom. "I used to practice every morning for hours," Kat said. "I've tried to hire morning babysitters to come be with the kids, but it just doesn't work the way it used to."

I asked Kat about what her practice had been and what she wanted it to be now and realized her answers were one and the same. When she was single, she'd woken up around 5:30 every morning, gone to her altar, lit candles and incense, meditated, done a Tarot reading for the day, practiced automatic writing, and then did forty-five minutes of yoga. This was before breakfast, even before coffee. ("Sometimes I let myself have a cup of green tea," she confessed.) That practice had reduced somewhat when she got together with her husband because he'd convinced her to sleep in until 8:00 on the weekends. She'd started practicing yoga in the evenings sometimes, too, and then she started putting that off. Once their first child was born, Kat needed a cup of coffee to even get out of bed. By the time her second was born her practice had dwindled to the occasional yoga class, and on rare occasions she'd burn some sage or pull a single card when both babies were miraculously asleep at the same time.

That was three kids ago. Today, Kat has five kids under seven. I realized in shock that she was holding the idea that to be "spiritual" as she once had been, she'd have to go back to the daily 5:30 a.m., caffeine-free, two-hour practice.

"Oh, Kat," I said. "Don't you see that you've graduated? It's time to up your game!" I explained that her life had moved on and her spiritual practice would have to, too. *"That's not a bad thing,"* I added, following the guidance I was hearing through clairaudience, "because your practice is ready to move on. The tools you need are available to you. You've just got to expand your mind to see it."

Our Guides are always upping our game, showing us how to access their wisdom in a way that works with our lives. I'm not saying we don't need to carve out time for practice—by all means, we do! But what that practice looks like evolves. It's meant to change over time—that isn't a flaw: it's a function. Our Guides want us to integrate our spirituality so seamlessly into our lives that it just feels natural.

"So what would feel natural to you, given your life as it is now?" I asked.

Kat thought hard. "Well, it would be nice to get a babysitter once a week to do that deep dive. Or at least some of it." She outlined how she could pack snacks and get the kids ready for the park, then send them out with the babysitter for about an hour and a half. When the littlest ones needed to come home for a nap, she could have the babysitter put them down in one of the upstairs bedrooms and hang with the other kids doing quiet activities like art and reading in the playroom beside it. "Then I could stay downstairs, in my room, and if I played some mantra music quietly, I probably wouldn't even hear them come home. That could get me a two and a half-hour stretch."

"That's great—actually that's quite a lot!" I encouraged. "And on the other days?"

"I could set my alarm for a half hour early and get myself up before the others—any day I don't wake up to a kid in the bed with me, that is," she said, laughing. "And then I could see what's possible. If the channeling comes easily, I could automatic write, and otherwise I could meditate."

"That sounds perfect," I said. "On top of that, grab any moment that you can to remind yourself who you are. Remember that it doesn't have to remain status quo, because we should all be looking to grow and expand our spiritual knowledge and practice. So if you have that five minutes in the shower, open the channel then. Don't be so rigid about it. Instead of having your spirituality in one hand and your life in the other, put them together." I demonstrated by holding my two fists to the sides, then opening my palms and bringing them together in prayer, mimicking what I saw in my third eye. "Let your spirituality into your life. It may seem like a detour from what you intended, but it's actually you moving up to the next level. Your Guides are showing you what's next."

Through our conversation, Kat considered what was possible in her life. The schedule she worked out is reasonable, given the constraints associated with being a mom of five—in fact, I think most moms would find it admirable and abundant. Kat's spiritual practice isn't going to look like what it used to during an earlier phase of her life, but by shifting her expectations of herself, she can still weave connection with Spirit into her days. And this is actually what Spirit wants for her.

When we look back on our journey, we'll see that the detours we took became the road itself. We may have intended to just cruise straight ahead; we may have seen all the brake lights and thought something was going wrong. But the truth is each time we adapted by taking a detour, we created the unique route that was perfect for us.

It isn't always easy to see this. Sometimes we need a little intervention, like what I offered Kat in our conversation. Kat needed a pit crew to get her back on the road, so I stepped up to help—just as I needed a pit crew when I felt stuck at the beginning of the pandemic, when Jane and Stephen set me up with Zoom. Let's take a look at the role our pit crew can take.

A Quick Refresh

Sometimes we need a pit stop: a chance for our crew of trusted friends to clean us up, swap out some old ideas and perspectives, and get us back on the road. This is our *soul pack*. Their souls have made contracts with ours, whether for our whole lives or for a fleeting moment, and we're meant to help each other learn what we came here to learn. Members of our soul pack can show up in many ways, but when they function as a pit crew, they help us celebrate our wins so we can keep going. None of us do this alone. Our Guides can identify for us the people we can trust when things get uncomfortable. They send us the exact people we need.

One of the biggest wins I had during the pandemic was selling my second book *Medium Mentor* to a publisher. Due to some shake-ups at the publishing house that put out *Believe, Ask, Act*, that book had been out of print for some time. In the publishing world, this is just about the worst thing that can happen. Most authors who experience that with a first book don't go on to sell a second one, even when (like me) it was completely out of their control. I was pretty worried this would happen to me. So when *Medium Mentor* found its publishing home, I was thrilled.

But then I did the financials and realized that, while I was still grateful the publisher was willing to take a chance on me, I wouldn't make enough in my advance to even cover the costs of writing and editing the project. I was actually going to lose money on the book! I had the capital to finance it, but I felt badly about the whole idea. I reached out to a dear friend who has been published many times to discuss it.

She didn't want to hear anything about the money. "That happens sometimes," she said, dismissing me immediately. "Let's focus on the real story here: YOU SOLD YOUR BOOK!" She shook her hands in the air, a huge smile on her face. "MaryAnn, that's incredible!" Her perspective was everything to me. It allowed me to drop my ego, tone down my fears, and get back to what really mattered.

My pit crew is made up of my closest friends and family—the people I really trust. There are other key members of my pit crew I have met in a professional capacity, too. I am lucky to have a doctor I can really trust, for instance. I also still communicate regularly with my first teacher of psychic mediumship, Pat. My Guides work through my pit crew to keep me well-oiled and squeaky-clean.

A whole lot of psychic mediumship is about showing up as part of the pit crew for others. This doesn't mean you have to read for others or even offer to do so. In our personal lives, most of the time the best way to offer channeled messages for others is through advice, as we speak up from the greatest good and for the highest good. Resist the urge to say more than you need to; even if it's just texting heart emojis at the perfect moment or saying a few words very intentionally, sharing messages for others is a powerful way for guidance to come through.

I remember an early experience with this when I reached out to a friend who had recently discovered she was pregnant. She was super-nervous about the pregnancy as she'd had close friends—including myself—go through losses. This was long before I had decided to develop my mediumship, so I didn't even know what I was channeling. I had a dream that I barely remembered; all I knew when I woke up was that I'd dreamed about her pregnancy. In my dream, the baby's name was Ben and Ben was dressed in red.

So I said rather offhandedly, "I had a dream about you last night. You were pregnant. The baby's name was Ben and Ben was dressed in red." I didn't try to interpret it or give it meaning; I didn't try to fill in the blanks (and there were many blanks!). Instead, I just passed on the exact pieces I remembered.

She gasped and stared at me. "My grandfather's name is Ben," she said, and then explained that he had been an observant Jew in life. "In the Jewish religion, putting a baby in red is good luck. It feels like that's a message from my grandfather telling me he's watching and offering me good luck." She found this greatly relieving.

It's important to note that I didn't have to do much—I only needed to pass on exactly what I'd been sent. By not putting myself in the interpretation, I gave her space to decipher the meaning on her own through her frame of reference. This is the best way to be part of a pit crew.

Pit stops are a powerful way to shift energy. Whenever you find yourself stuck—or even careening out of control—you can call out to your Guides, "I need a pit stop! Please send my crew!" Then sit back and wait to see what they provide. It may be in the form of someone else or a dream or intuition or a synchronistic experience. Spirit is very creative and always finds ways to work through the world around us to bring us what we need.

Part of Spirit's work is to clear the space we need to keep moving forward, and our Guides' job is to show us where that space is. Whether it's a detour, a pit stop, or any other small intervention, these experiences help us contextualize the traffic jams that appear to keep us from moving forward. Seeing minor setbacks this way works to move us from the fear that things are going wrong into the confidence that everything is going exactly right.

Even when we don't have a strong pit crew in the physical world, we can reach out to our pit crew in the spiritual realm: our Guides! While it's useful to have a spiritual hotline through the people close to us, they can also connect with us directly. It's best to make this a habit though, so that our Guides have regular opportunities to get through to us.

When the road ahead is blocked or needs a detour, our role is to stay open, stay positive, and reach out for help as needed. We can always look for what our Guides are sending us and offer a little gratitude, even if we can't make much sense of it at the time. If you're reading these words and you're in an especially tough moment, please let this be the pit stop you need! It doesn't take long to shift our perspective back to the positive again; a new way of seeing things can arrive almost instantly.

EXERCISE: HABITUAL CHECK-IN

One of the most powerful practices I've found to ease life's challenges is scheduling a regular check-in meeting with my Guides and making it a habit.

If you haven't picked it up by now, I encourage you to make this as chatty and informal as you need it to be. You can choose a symbolic gesture to start with each time, such as lighting a candle or saying a specific prayer, but make it something simple that you can easily incorporate into your life without much fanfare. Then, as always, it's best to end the session with gratitude; gratitude brings us to the highest vibrations where miracles occur.

To make sure this really becomes habit, you can program an alarm into your phone to remind you to do it at least to start. It may also help to attach it to another regular weekly event. You may want to wake up one morning a week and do a small practice with your cup of coffee or add the practice in after a weekly event you already attend. This idea, known as *habit stacking*, has been used by numerous behavior experts to help build new habits. It's simple: pick something you already do largely without fail, and make sure you implement your new habit every time. Boom! A new habit is formed.

Once you've picked the time and date or event to trigger your weekly check-in and chosen a symbolic gesture to start with, you're ready to go.

First, call your Guides. This can be as simple as whispering out loud, "Hey guys, it's time for our check-in!" (You can also choose to be formal—something like, "Beloved Guides, with gratitude and reverence, I call you to this place to meet with me now." There's nothing wrong with formality; it just isn't how I do it, personally!) Once you feel the presence of your Guides, start to review what's happening in your life this week. What's working? What isn't? What did you discuss last week, and how are things going since you had that discussion? If you made any commitments to take action, how did you hold to them (or not)? Which manifestations came to fruition this week, and which ones are still processing?

Then allow your Guides to lead you toward your lessons for the week. What are you not seeing? What could you understand more clearly? What do you need from your Guides—what requests do you have for them? What opportunities, conversations, signs, etc., are you manifesting outside of yourself? And most importantly of all, what actions can you take to shift your role in the process? Like any good business meeting, try to finish it with one or two actionable to-dos, and if you can, write them down so you don't forget.

If you've made requests of your Guides or are manifesting things, be sure to set it and forget it. Resist the urge to try to take forcible actions on these things or put too much focus on them; believe that they will come and release them to the Universe.

To end the session, offer your Guides gratitude. This can be a feeling, a friendly "Thanks! Catch ya later!" or a more formal benediction that recognizes the value of their help. Whatever you do, be sure to end your check-in feeling good.

Then get to work taking action where you need to take action. Remember, your human life is a co-creation between yourself and your Guides. Your participation is mandatory. And that is its own blessing.

Chapter 9
ROAD RAGE!

Love and light!

Trust the Universe!

For the highest and greatest good! Always!

I'LL GO AHEAD AND SAY IT: IT ALL GETS A LITTLE BIT ANNOYING sometimes!

As a spiritualist, these same words have passed my lips many times over. But they're the last thing we need to hear when we're right in the middle of our very human stuff. Yes, we are all put on this planet to learn, and yes, we are all gifted with strong inner guidance to help us do so. I believe in that so wholeheartedly that I've dedicated this entire book to teaching it. And yet, we are human—extremely human. Sometimes even painfully human. That humanity comes with the good, the bad, and the *way* ugly.

I believe in the perfection of all things. Lest you retch a little, let me explain: that means that even our perceived flaws are divine. We were designed to be exactly as we are. Nothing about us is an accident. That includes our anger, our rage, our resistance, our envy, our drama—all of it.

It took me years to realize I was never going to pray away the tough persona I'd come to embody in my teen years. All the love and light in the world couldn't shut her down, and eventually I realized it just isn't supposed to! I am equal parts spiritual and scrappy, and I won't apologize for that because it's who I am. This understanding was hard-won—it took time, and acceptance, and generally blowing off a lot of the rhetoric I'd heard in the spiritual world. It took putting down my ideals and embracing myself as I am.

And a funny thing happened when I did that: when I accepted and welcomed everything about myself, it became a lot easier to accept and welcome the world as it is. I stopped fighting myself so hard, and I stopped fighting my life so hard.

I'd like to share this understanding with you because I suspect there are parts of you that you've worried you'll never overcome. It's time to stop worrying, because not only will you likely not overcome them, but there is no benefit in doing so. Instead, the true benefits come when we work with the exact personality we've been given, bringing *all of it* to this journey and allowing it to guide us. Yes, that includes the ugly stuff, right there along with the pretty nice stuff.

This chapter is all about integrating that ugly stuff so it can be part of your process. Some people call this integrating the shadow. The shadow is the not-so-savory parts of our ego that we would rather never bring out into the light. In these pages you'll find permission—and even encouragement—to be exactly who you are, because it's *all* part of the spiritual path. Your Guides can help you incorporate every part of yourself and use it for good. So rev your engine! Put on your toughest face! It's time to celebrate everything that makes us human. It's time to road rage.

Spiritualists, Not Saints

We've all got our thing, right? That one situation that just pisses us off again and again.

While I've used driving as a metaphor throughout this book, it's time to admit something uncomfortable: I sometimes suffer from literal road rage. As in, I sometimes lose it completely when I'm driving a car.

To be clear, I'm not an extreme road rager. I don't get out of my car to fight with anyone or let it affect the safety of my driving. But I have been known to yell at other drivers behind my own closed windows. I get all kinds of pissed off when people's poor choices make traffic into a mess.

I remember one time, way back when I was working in fashion retail, when I had had a terrible morning. Someone cut me off; someone else drove way under the speed limit; and no fewer than three people pushed through yellow lights in ways I was sure they shouldn't have. By the time I got to my store I was significantly worked up. I started relating my morning to my colleague in colorful language: "This person was tailgating me, what an asshole! And this person, total asshole! Then this asshole over here . . ."

My colleague cut me off. "MaryAnn, if there are that many assholes on the road, maybe you should consider whether *you're* the asshole?" She laughed nervously, hoping I'd take the joke.

I did. In fact, I burst out laughing. "Huh . . . maybe I am," I answered.

Her statement has stuck with me for years. Maybe I *am* the asshole—or maybe I should at least consider it. I think it's always worth considering whether we are the creators of at least some of our own problems. That doesn't have to be a bad thing. When we see a good number of our problems as challenges—opportunities to learn something our soul has committed to figuring out—it stands to reason that we would subconsciously call some of these challenges to ourselves. Not all of them, obviously—sometimes we are all victims of forces outside of our control. Tragic things happen, and life can be unfair. But we can also be the asshole in traffic, or one of the many assholes. Understanding and even embracing this is part of our spiritual work.

That's right—it's completely spiritual to stand in our own imperfection and know that it, too, is perfect. We are spiritualists, not saints. We're not supposed to be any different than we are. We're just supposed to start exactly where we stand right now and grow from there.

I was born on the South Shore of Long Island, New York, as part of the third generation of a very Italian American family. I loved growing up on Long Island surrounded by warm, loving, and entirely unapologetic people who were brave enough to tell you what they thought. My elders fought with each other in Italian—loudly. I don't know what they were saying, but I do know they had zero issue letting each other in on what the problem was. I was surrounded by big personalities, and I fit right in. I grew up feeling confident about who I was, doing a lot of stage work, acting and singing, and frequently performing for my family. I was outgoing in school and easily putting myself out there.

But as I grew older, I was criticized for being "too much." In response, I started to hold back. I began deferring to the needs of others, worried that being confident made me too dominant. While I always stayed true to that feisty girl, I often found myself trying to tone her down so I could seem nicer and more docile.

I now see that I spent most of my five decades wrapped up in people-pleasing. I'd please my family with one set of behaviors, and I'd please the outside world with another. Both came from the true me, but I didn't trust that I could be fully natural; I didn't trust that the right part of me would come out at the right time. Instead of embracing both parts of me, I made myself small inside both of these images, apologizing for myself. Looking back, I can see that people-pleasing didn't do anyone any favors. When I was in my good-girl persona, I was nice, but I don't know that I was always kind. And when I was sassy for the sake of it, I may have come across as mean.

I don't have time or energy for any of that anymore. Especially now, with the wisdom of age—thank you menopause!—I feel far less compelled to make everyone comfortable. I want to be kind and compassionate, and I also want to be tough when needed—but I want both of those parts of me to emerge naturally, in response to an inner calling instead of a desire to please. My Guides have led me here step-by-step over the course of five decades. They've taught me to catch myself more and more quickly when I'm engaging in people-pleasing, and in response I've become even more authentic and real. Acting from a balanced and genuine place allows me to be much more accessible to the people around me, and most importantly, it opens my heart to myself. It takes about one-tenth of the effort I expended on living up to what I thought people wanted, and the benefits are exponential.

Today, I try to let my inner sass have her space without allowing her to lead the way completely. She keeps me from being messed with in ways that I don't like. She helps me hold my own. When I channel her to fight the good fight, she can be my ally instead of my adversary. And simultaneously, I push myself to let my compassionate and loving nature show without fear. I've learned that a little vulnerability doesn't make me weak, but instead gives me a base to work from. I've found balance—and it's made me a better person. Figuring out how to do this is part of my spiritual work.

I bring this to you because I want to know: what's *your* spiritual work? What do you have hanging out there in the dark, well away from the love and light you hope to bring to the world? And what can you do with it? When we seek guidance around these questions, we find ways to let our shadow serve the light, and we get the confidence to do so without apologizing.

I've written about anger here because it's the strongest aspect of my shadow. It's important for all of us to seek out anger, because we all have it. There are other substantial shadow emotions too, though, such as envy and resentment. Leading a guided life means we must explore all of them. Whatever is strongest in our personality is there for a reason. It doesn't mean we can just let those impulses fly and harm others—it's one thing to yell behind our closed windows, and it's quite another to pull over and punch someone in the face. When channeled appropriately, though, the shadow has the ability to serve us in ways that are 100 percent spiritual.

Isn't it reassuring to know that we don't have to be saints? When I discuss this in my workshops, I notice that most people are a little hesitant to own their darkness, but they're relieved at the same time. Notice that relief, because it's one way our Guides demonstrate what's meant for us. Fighting ourselves is an enormous energy drain, and as of this exact moment, I give you permission to stop doing that. Instead, let's look at how the heavy stuff can serve us.

We'll start with considering how it can help us discern what is right for us and what isn't.

What Doesn't Resonate

OK, so while I'm doling out permissions, let's consider this one:

> *You are always free to throw away what has been served to you. It could be a reading, or advice, or even a card you pull from your deck. You can throw out parts of this book—just rip out the pages, go ahead! You officially have permission to say, "That doesn't feel like it's in alignment," "That doesn't resonate," or even, "I don't receive that." Anytime, anywhere.*

It's normal to have our ego balk at certain things—ideas, people, etc. And sometimes, that's an invitation to harness our free will, to let that idea in deeper or befriend that person. But there's no need to overdo it, because sometimes our ego is spot-on. Sometimes our balking at something or someone is actually our higher wisdom speaking out.

Just as we can use our free will to set boundaries with others, we can also use it to set boundaries with the spiritual information we take in. One of the reasons I fix bad readings is that I don't believe Spirit ever sends us negative or painful messages; Spirit surely challenges us, but our Guides are there to help us find the most positive, helpful, and affirming interpretation available. So a "bad" reading is really just a poor interpretation by the medium receiving the information. In any case, as psychics, we are always free to tell Spirit to rephrase things in a way that is easier to interpret positively, and if we go to a psychic or psychic medium to get a reading, we are always welcome to say, "I don't receive what you're saying." This is how we fine-tune our claircognizance.

The great news is that we can't mess it up. Even when we turn in the exact opposite direction from where our Guides want us to go—using our free will to resist what Spirit has to say—they'll lead us forward from there.

Our resistance, in other words, is part of the process. It isn't contrary to what's happening—it's part of it. It's instructive. Bring it on.

My student Sandra, a website designer who has studied both Tarot and personality typing systems, learned this when she was backpacking in India and was offered a reading by another traveler. He called himself a teacher, but he seemed more like a cult leader, albeit of a very small cult. "There were several women working for him I really liked, so even though I wasn't that impressed by him, I was impressed by them," Sandra explained. "One of them became my friend, and she went on and on about how great her teacher was. And then he offered to trade a Tarot reading for some work on his website, and while I'm open to trades, it brought up all this resistance. But he was really pushy about it, and my friend told me he was just this incredible Tarot reader. Finally I said, 'Whatever, it's worth a shot to hear what he has to say,' so I scheduled the reading," she said.

Sandra went into the reading with an open mind, but she wasn't that impressed by what he had to say. She could tell that the person reading her was getting a lot from a personality typing system she already knew well. "He was saying all these things—that I struggle with envy, with comparing myself to other people—and it was all true, but these are things I already knew about myself. So I kept saying, 'Yeah, I hear you, I'm working on that,' not in a defensive way but just kind of collaborating with the reading as it was happening. Then about an hour into it he got kind of annoyed. He said my ego was too strong." Sandra perked up because she always welcomed an opportunity to see her ego from a new angle, so she asked to hear more about what he was perceiving. "That's when he said, 'I can tell you aren't taking any of this in because you haven't started to cry. Most people are crying by now.' 'What?!' I thought, 'Ew! What kind of a reader is hell-bent on making people cry?' " Something about the situation felt really off, and Sandra had a strong compulsion to cut and run. But she didn't want to have a big ego and didn't want to disappoint her new friend, so she stayed.

Sandra tried to explain herself and how, since she already knew these aspects of herself and was working on them, they hadn't hit deeply enough to make her cry. "Plus, I don't think crying always means you're doing the work," she explained to me. "It *can* mean that, but not necessarily." Finally, she realized she was being guided to just say no to this guy. And that's when she realized it was part of a greater lesson for her.

"I thought back to all these men I hadn't said no to—spiritual teachers, boyfriends, bosses, etc. And I was just like, 'No dude. I know who I am; I know what I'm doing; and it's time for me to go.' " Sandra told him the reading was complete and left. And she learned a big lesson: that sometimes, her resistance *is* her higher wisdom.

There are plenty of people out there who would agree with the Tarot reader in this story—that if Sandra were really doing her work, she would have cried. But the same situation can also be read the opposite way: Sandra needed to learn to say no, and her resistance was her ally in that moment. Sandra is the only one who knows her own truth. She listened to her guidance and read it the way she read it, regardless of what her new friend thought of her.

Part of this process of spiritual growth is learning to take what's going to work for us and separate out what isn't. Our anger, our resistance, the giant "No!" within us can help us do this. At every turn, our Guides can lead us to see what kind of no needs to be worked through and what kind of no is actually our inner guidance.

So how do we give ourselves this permission to discern? It starts with allowing ourselves to ignore what other people may think. Sandra didn't want to disappoint her new friend. She didn't want the Tarot reader to think her ego was out of control. But she had to accept both these things to learn her lesson; she had to follow what her Guides were telling her, not what the humans around her were saying.

It also helps to lower the stakes by forgiving ourselves for any mistakes we might make in the process of uncovering our true path.

Feeling the Feels

In working with hundreds of students and grieving families over the years, I've seen the power that feelings like regret and resentment have over our spiritual process. They can create massive roadblocks. As I wrote in the previous chapter, roadblocks and detours always become a part of the road. Yet it's also true that sometimes our lesson is to bust right through them.

Forgiveness has the power to do this. It is one of humanity's greatest collective lessons, which is why so many loved ones speak about it from the Other Side. Forgiveness is the pebble of change that starts a ripple effect throughout our lives.

About now you may be thinking, ***This is all well and good, but please MaryAnn, don't tell me that when I'm super-angry or down I need to forgive.*** Well, on some level you do—but you don't need to start with anyone else or with the situation you're in, because that's the hardest part! Instead, I suggest forgiving yourself for being super-angry or down. This is a crucial way to connect with the energy even amid your challenge.

Suppressing our more difficult emotions is very dangerous. It can cause so many problems throughout our life—mental, physical, emotional, and of course, spiritual. We need to let ourselves feel them all the way, and only through that effort can we release these emotions. Often, the first step in doing this is to forgive ourselves for experiencing these feelings in the first place. Self-forgiveness gives us the space we need to feel our emotions. And when felt completely, our emotions serve a major purpose by helping us to work through our shadow. In fact, resistance to feeling emotions is often the thing that prevents us from embracing who we truly are—specifically the unsavory parts. When we feel our feelings all the way through, something breaks free.

All of our emotions are there for a reason. They point us to the memories, judgments, and experiences we haven't processed fully and therefore still need our attention. This is part of the reason I want to point you toward anger, which can be one of the loudest emotions.

Anger often shows us what is out of alignment in our lives. It can also illuminate an unmet need. Sometimes, we need to accept something we haven't accepted. That doesn't always mean we need to accept something that is unfair—sometimes, what we need to accept is that it's unfair! With a tragic death, for instance, our anger (which is a natural part of grief) isn't there to show us we need to accept that our person has been taken away; it's trying to tell us we need to accept how much we are resisting the fact that our person has been taken away. We don't need to be at peace with it; we need to be mad! We need to love the part of us that screams, "No, this is not OK with me!"

Being human is hard. Sometimes the best we can do is pray, stay connected to our higher power, and keep conversing with our Guides, *while* we rage about the things we don't understand. The world is supposed to have contrast. There are meant to be things we can accept and things we cannot. That doesn't mean we're doing something wrong.

This has been a big lesson for me, because allowing myself to feel my feelings isn't always easy. I'd rather just move through them quickly. (This is where my inner tough girl *doesn't* serve me and needs to be put in check; she can be hardened to a fault.)

For instance, a few years ago my friend Nico collaborated with me on a television show that really excited us both. I've heard many times that television will be a part of my path, helping me spread the message I've been called to bring to an even wider audience—though I will say, the one thing Guides can't tell us anything about is timing. Nico and I worked with a great production company and were thrilled with the pilot we created—even more so when we sold it!

Not long after, we heard that though the company that bought the pilot had liked it, they had chosen not to develop it into a series as we'd hoped. Some part of me suspected this might happen, but I also sometimes struggle to really let myself enter the darkness for fear I might end up there forever. So when Nico told me about it, my answer was very flat: "OK, that's fine." He pushed me a little on it. "It's OK to mourn it, you know," he said gently. "We worked hard. I'm disappointed. You can be, too."

Looking back, I can see that since it's only a television show, I didn't want to let myself be too wrapped up in my feelings of disappointment and loss. I felt ashamed to care too much, so I didn't let myself care at all. But I did care—I wasn't devastated, but I was legitimately disappointed. And I ended up hanging on to the experience far longer than I had to because I was afraid of experiencing that disappointment.

Ironically, it was allowing myself to feel the frustration in its full depth that released me of the emotion completely. That's how emotions work: when we avoid feeling them in their entirety, we actually end up feeling them for longer and suffering as a result. When we just feel them, we get out of the cycle. We set ourselves free.

The mind is one of the greatest emotional blockers. It seeks to rationalize any way it can—in this case, by telling me it was shameful to feel disappointed—which gets in the way of the process that needs to take place. As soon as rationality enters the picture, emotion is compromised.

I can see this when I look back on my grandmother's death. My mother's mother, Adelina, died when I was seventeen. She had been fighting colon cancer for quite some time, and it was clear she was near the end. One day my father showed up where I worked to tell me she had died and to take me home. I don't remember much about that day, except that on the drive home, I was so frozen my father said to me, "It's OK if you want to cry," and I responded, "It's not like I didn't expect it; it's OK." When we arrived at my mom's house, he let me out of the car, and I walked, perfectly composed, to the front door. I shut the door behind me and burst into tears. I couldn't share my grief with him; I just had to be alone.

Nearly forty years later, Nico gave me an opportunity to revisit this way of thinking. His saying, "It's OK to mourn," was so like my father's! I realized I wasn't letting myself really feel the depth of my sadness, especially not publicly. My mind was coming into the picture as a form of protection, rationalizing things to distract me from what hurt. Once I let myself have a pity party about the show, I was surprised to see it actually went pretty quickly. Feeling my feelings all the way allowed me to release them.

The truth is, nothing about our emotions needs to be rational. The sooner we can abandon that idea, the better. Then we can just feel our feelings before brushing ourselves off, rising up, and continuing down our road. Since the disappointment with the TV show, I've learned to do this much more effectively.

Over the past year, I put this strategy into action when it was finally time to put down my dog Phoenix. I was ready for it, but that didn't make it hurt any less. I lay with him on his bed, holding his head on my lap and snuggling him as we said goodbye. I let myself lose it completely, with the vet and my family watching as I first let him go and then lay there sobbing. A younger version of me would have looked at this as weakness, because I allowed myself to fall apart. But today, I know that we need to let ourselves fall apart sometimes.

Lil' Miss South Shore helps me do this with anger. She lets it out completely without shame or fear, and by the time I get out of my car, I'm ready to have a good day. I'm learning to do it with grief and sadness, too. When we forgive ourselves for our feelings and just let them out, we find we don't have to reside in them forever; we don't need to keep reliving the situation that hurt us; we don't need to hold on to things. And if we do hold on to things, we can forgive ourselves for that, too.

When we do this, we find that forgiving others and/or situations follows naturally. I suggest putting effort into forgiving yourself and feeling your feelings. But forgiving things external to you is not necessarily something you *do*; it's more like something that ***happens***. Give space for this and see what comes.

The exercise that follows is geared at helping you do that. It may be one you repeat again and again—and if it is, please know that I'm right there with you! Learning to forgive so we can feel is a process that takes time. It's an important theme that will come up over and over along the road of life as we learn to embrace everything about who we are. As always, our Guides will show us the way.

EXERCISE: GUIDED FORGIVENESS

For this writing exercise, you will need a pen and paper or a notebook. You may also type on a device, though I personally still love the old-school method of pen and paper.

Cleanse and ground yourself to start.

Then make a list of things you are struggling with in life right now. It could be anything: as big as the loss of a loved one or as small as someone cutting you off in traffic.

Now call your Guides in to help you. See or feel a Guide holding your hand. Let them know you'll need their assistance and feel their supportive presence. It may also help to bring in a loved one to support you, as loved ones are great at working with forgiveness.

Then consider the first item on your list.

Watch the situation or issue play out in front of your eyes like you're watching a movie screen. Then ask your Guide: "Have I forgiven myself completely for everything I feel in association with this?" If not, take the time to call in self-forgiveness.

Then ask your Guide, "How can I forgive others for this situation or issue?" You may or may not be able to do it yet, but let your Guide show you where forgiveness could help.

Move on to the next item on your list.

Go through the whole list this way! If you have a long list, you may want to split this over several sessions.

Be prepared for your Guides to give you a beautiful pep talk in this process—a quick pit stop to give you some perspective. You may be faced with impatience with yourself for not forgiving, and that's fine—as your Guides will tell you! What's most important is you're showing up to do the work.

When you're complete, thank your Guide and yourself. Then write down what you experienced. What could you see you had already forgiven? What were you able to forgive today? And what did you wish to forgive, but were unable to at this time?

Revisit this page in a few days and see if there's anything else to release.

Chapter 10
REARVIEW MIRROR

I'VE WRITTEN FREQUENTLY IN THESE PAGES ABOUT BOTH accountability and gratitude. No matter what we encounter along the road, the least useful thing we can do is develop resentment. Things are the way they are, and we are all ultimately accountable for how we face the things that take place in our lives. We can always find something to be grateful for, and doing so brings us to the highest vibrational realm.

That sounds nice and ideal, you may be thinking, ***but how on earth do I get there?***

My Guides have shown me that the answer lies in understanding our lives in their greater context: as part of a process of spiritual awakening that takes place over many lifetimes. The reason there is no end point to this particular road trip is that we are, in fact, continuously on the journey toward Spirit. The adventure doesn't end when our bodies die. In the context of our soul, this single lifetime is a blip, a tiny fraction of time.

In the process, we are learning life lessons through the events that take place and our experience of them as human beings. These lessons add up to greater contracts our souls have made with the Universe in the space between lives.

Though I've mentioned these terms intermittently throughout this book, this chapter explains them in full detail. Waiting until now to share it with you was an intentional decision. It takes working through some of our stuff with our Guides at our side to be ready to really understand these concepts. I wanted to be sure you were in good connection with your own guidance before presenting this to you, because all I can do is explain it as best as I understand it; it's your own Guides who can help to ground the truth of these concepts in your life and in your heart.

The commencement of any spiritual awakening is an intense experience. It's necessary to go to these depths, but it isn't comfortable. Therefore,

I suggest we start at the low point, the one that may be hardest to digest and likely marks the most significant part of your spiritual experience this lifetime.

And lest you think you're alone in probing these depths, I will start by revealing my own.

Unraveling

I'm not sure if I'll be the first to tell you this, but someone's got to do it:

Spiritual awakenings are damn hard.

People get excited around the idea of a spiritual awakening. "*Ooohhh*," we think, with some sort of angelic music swirling in our head, "*aaaahhhh*," swelling to a crescendo as light breaks through the golden clouds. Perhaps we imagine we'll be wandering through the woods barefoot in a long, flowy gown under the full moon, charging our crystals and building natural altars, assisted by friendly forest animals like we're Cinderella getting dressed for the ball. Or perhaps we see our enlightenment as a little edgier, concentrating as a beam of light pierces our third eye and splinters into multicolored fractals, our physical eyes opening wide because we finally *see*.

It's true that the end result of a spiritual awakening may look like that—at least somewhat. But while we're in them, real spiritual awakenings are nothing like that idealized vision. At the heart of every real spiritual awakening is an unraveling. They are the lowest point of our lives, when we realize that the way we have been looking at things will no longer carry us forward. And yes, they do bring us some of that angelic *aaaahhhh*, as they give us gratitude for nature and life and the people we love and remind us to turn our face to the sunlight and feel the breeze, enjoying being present in the moment. But the overwhelming experience of an awakening is also like being punched in the gut. Suddenly we look at ourselves in all our beautiful ugliness and realize, *Oh wow, I have been doing life all wrong. I haven't dealt with this aspect of myself, and I simply can't go on without addressing it. I can see the role I've been playing and how I've been in a deep sleep. I have so much work to do!* It's devastating. It's terrifying. But something in it is electric, and without knowing exactly how, we find the will to keep going. Then, if the awakening is complete, the only thing we can do in that moment is grab whatever tools we can find and get to work.

When we finally wake up, we'll be able to see it all clearly and understand the pivotal role each moment has played in our development. We'll perceive the bigger picture and understand much more about what we came here to do, why particular moments were so hard for us, and why we resisted what our Guides were trying to tell us about them. But in the moment we experience them, we don't have this clarity, and it isn't easy at all.

This chapter is about that context: the greater process our souls are going through as they evolve, and the role this particular lifetime plays within that evolution. Like so many things in this book, it isn't a one-and-done experience. Instead, it's a process of understanding that takes time. Each challenge we face is an opportunity for our Guides to show us what this lifetime is all about.

To demonstrate this, it's time for me to tell you about what was—and I hope continues to be—the hardest thing I've been through in this lifetime. I've resisted writing about it in any detail until this point. Now, twenty-five years after it happened, I'm finally ready.

When my second pregnancy ended in loss, I only let myself crumble once. Just once.

It was in the kitchen. Everything in that house was a shade of beige: taupe tiles, sandy brown cabinets. I felt my knees hit that tile, hard, and from there I just melted until I lay on the floor, unable to breathe, my body racked with silent sobs. We'd had a few dicey days and had finally accepted that, under the circumstances, there was no way we could bring this baby to term. To call what I experienced grief is not enough. Such a level of emotion doesn't fit into a single word. It was shock; it was guilt; it was an acute sense of failure. And it was not just that I had failed my child, but that I *was* a failure in every sense of the word—that everything about my life was a failure.

I'm not someone who lets herself fall apart. I don't hit the floor sobbing—I appreciate people who experience things like that, but it just isn't me. And yet there I was, cheek pressed against that drab taupe surface, shuddering and broken, my side grazing against the floor with each ragged breath. To this day, I look back on this moment as the single most horrifying event of my entire life. My first husband walked in then; he saw me like that. He's the only one who ever did. Once I picked myself up, I was made of steel.

The following days were filled with pain: physical pain, emotional pain, spiritual pain. At one point, I was at the doctor's office and ran into another woman with a situation similar to my own. She looked like I felt: exhausted, shocked, broken. "How are you . . . like that?" she asked, waving her hands at me to indicate what she meant. I was dressed to the nines, almost freakishly composed. My nails were on point, hair done, makeup in place. My moment in the kitchen was over. I didn't need to do that anymore. "I have to be like this," I answered. "I have a one-year-old daughter. She needs me."

A few days later it was my birthday. A well-meaning friend, knowing what had just happened and wanting to focus on the positive, sent me flowers and balloons. I remember how I crushed the flowers as I pushed them into the garbage can, how I popped the balloons one by one. There would be no celebration of any kind during this moment of mourning; *how dare she even suggest such a thing*, I thought.

Though this occurred years before I started my formal psychic training, I had already known to steel myself for a difficult experience in this pregnancy. I'd had a dream early on that told me something wasn't right. Also when it was revealed I was carrying another girl, I became suspicious because I'd always known I'd have a girl and a boy. I was devastated when things started going wrong nonetheless; it was very much a wanted pregnancy. Instead of pausing to really feel it, though, I pushed through my emotional distress, using it to drive me forward toward my next move, which was bringing my next child into the world. I knew he was waiting for me, and that knowing helped me believe everything was, on some level, OK. I could move on.

Looking back, I was so young. I didn't know how to handle the experience other than by torturing myself. I didn't give myself time to grieve. I didn't give myself grace to be messy and imperfect. In the twenty-five years since then, I have worked with hundreds of people who have lost family members and dozens who lost pregnancies and even living children. I would never dream of holding them to the standard to which I held myself. I encourage people to mourn fully and completely, even though (or perhaps because) when it was my turn, I couldn't let myself. I was too wrapped up in people-pleasing and in what I thought it meant to be a woman and a mother. I was too focused on parenting my living child.

I can also accept that, to some extent, my priorities were in order: I *did* need to parent my child. But I also needed to mourn. I look back on the girl I was and wish I could just hold her and let her unravel. But beyond that one moment on the kitchen floor, she didn't; she couldn't. And that's part of my story I'll carry forever.

Life is a complex thing, though, and this moment was no different. To some degree, something necessary was happening. I had a one-year old daughter and I knew my son was waiting for me, so I went back to my faith to push forward.

I remember a poignant conversation I had during that time with my paternal grandmother Anne. She was an incredible woman and a devout Catholic. She had lost her own daughter at the age of twenty-seven to cancer and her husband, my grandfather, early enough that I never met him. Despite facing such enormous challenges and grief, she was one of the most beautiful, optimistic people I've ever known; a woman of enormous faith and love for God. I remember the way she looked me in the eyes and spoke words so wise they have stayed with me ever since:

"MaryAnn, please don't be mad at God."

"I'm not mad at God," I answered, and I instantly knew it was true.

I want to be clear with you right now: being mad at God is OK. It's a part of grief. But it's also OK to grieve without feeling that kind of anger. And though I think I could have definitely mourned my loss more fully, being mad at God just wasn't part of my story.

Feeling everything that came with that loss *was* a part of my story, however. It took years to work through the emotions, which came to the surface and healed in bits and pieces over time. In fact, they're still coming to the surface now, as I'll tell you in the chapters to come.

Just recently, twenty-five years after my unraveling on the kitchen floor, I was having a conversation with someone when I heard myself make oblique reference to the fact that I hadn't lost a child. My Guides piped up immediately: ***But MaryAnn, you*** have ***lost a child.*** It was the first time it had dawned on me in that way. While I still can't know the heartbreak that parents of living children experience when their children die, there are aspects of their experience I can relate to my own. This is true, just as it is true that I didn't get mad at God. Navigating grief often calls us to hold a good deal of complexity like this.

I am blessed to possess a faith that just doesn't budge, no matter what I throw at it. That's how I was born. That's part of my lesson in this lifetime: that faith, for me, is simple. I don't work at maintaining it. It's just there. I'm not right, and no one whose faith shakes is wrong. We are just here for different reasons. We are all on the road toward spiritual awakening, and nearly all those awakenings will involve some degree of unraveling. Along the way, we have different lessons to learn.

Lessons for Each Lifetime

Each of us has a soul that came here to learn specific lessons. We chose these lessons in the space between lives.

I once heard this process described in an interview by someone who had a near-death experience. Betty Guadagno, who speaks frequently about her experience on numerous podcasts as well as her own social media channels, shifted from atheist to spiritualist after an overdose that took her to that space between lives. There, before deciding to come back, she pulled life lessons down from the shelves one by one. This imagery shows us how much choice is involved: yes, we have to choose certain lessons to learn, but we are the ones who make the ultimate decision of what those lessons will be. I love this visual so much that I adapted it as part of the exercise at the end of this chapter.

In processing the loss of my pregnancy, I've found many life lessons. I have had to work on people-pleasing and perfectionism. I've had the opportunity to sit with many people in their grief, and doing so has shown me how much I denied my own. In other moments, I've seen how I managed to process my grief over time without developing resentment, which is a blessing to me. I've come to realize that it's impossible to have everything ideal or perfect, and I've learned that having my world shattered is something I can survive. I found out exactly how strong I am.

There are also plenty of events we will never understand fully in this life. Sometimes, we're meant to simply feel defeated by the challenges we experience, because the lesson for us is to completely release the idea that we will ever learn anything positive from them. If you're reading this and you've been through something truly impossible, you may even feel angry at what I am saying; you may not *want* to derive any positive meaning (or any meaning at all) from what has happened in your life—and it is true that some things do just happen. What makes something a life lesson is not the magnitude of the experience, but the significance we attach to it.

From that perspective, we can see that our life lessons don't really have that much to do with the events in our lives at all. While they are *initiated* by life events, the lessons themselves are much more about the emotions we experience because of those events. The daughter I carried who was never born did not come to this earth to teach me a lesson; that kind of thinking is both wrong and harmful. Instead, I took that experience as an opportunity to learn about things like perfectionism, people-pleasing, and faith—not by choice, but because my emotional experience led me there.

Your own unraveling can come from something big or small. Sometimes, really big events—even tragic ones—don't become part of our life lessons, because they're simply really big, tragic events. On the other hand, sometimes something small ends up throwing us way off-kilter and becomes part of our life lesson.

When I explained this to my student Jay, he laughed. "I can relate," he said, and went on to tell me about how he'd been rear-ended at a traffic light. The other driver stayed in her car, smiled and waved, and drove away before Jay could get her license plate number. Jay pulled over and saw that his car had a small dent on the bumper—nothing big, and since he often parked it on the street, it was hardly even noticeable next to the other dents and scratches. "But it pissed me off so, so much," Jay recounted. "Like too much. I just couldn't let it go. I was thinking about it all the time." He went to great lengths to figure out who had done it, asking two businesses on the corner for their CCTV footage and posting in local groups online. "It was like two months," Jay said, shaking his head. "If you talked to me during that time, I basically wouldn't have told you about anything else. Holding her accountable was the only thing I thought about."

Jay never did figure out who had rear-ended him. But eventually, his wife pointed out that his obsession with it was becoming unhealthy and suggested, though the other driver was in the wrong, Jay was responsible for his response. This conversation triggered something in Jay, and he started to do his own work around the issue. He realized that he was locked up in fear, wanting to control the actions of others so the world could be a safe and predictable place, and that his reaction felt eerily familiar. He started to connect different events throughout his life and saw that while it was the first time he'd been in that kind of a situation, his feelings around it were much older. "I mean, it wasn't cool that she did that, but my wife was right—someone else might have let that go more easily than I did. In the end, that only happened when I took responsibility for what it was bringing up for me," Jay said. Eventually, Jay even moved into a space of gratitude—not for having been rear-ended, but for having the opportunity to work through one of his life lessons.

As Jay's experience demonstrates, the external event that brings the life lesson to the surface is not the point—it can be as big as the loss of a child or as small as a fender bender. The only role the external event plays in this process is to dislodge something within us, giving us space to deal with the emotions we agreed to come here and face in this lifetime.

So how do we know the difference between an event that simply happens at random and one that is part of our life lessons? Developing and trusting in our claircognizance, or inner knowing, is key here. One way I'm usually tipped off that I'm dealing with a life lesson is when I start to hear my own thoughts repeating on a loop—a familiar loop, one I've played a thousand times before. The more we can attune ourselves to observing those thoughts from a distance—not only not engaging with them but actually becoming a little bored by them—the more we can work toward our own healing.

Learning the lessons our soul is bringing us is a multistep process. Working with our Guides eases that process. They won't do the work for us, but they will always lead us to the *who, what, when, where,* and *why* of our emotional experiences—*who* was involved, including in past lives or much earlier in this life; *what* we felt on a deeper level; *when* this all started; *where* we were when it started, both literally and figuratively in our lives; and *why* have we attached the feelings we have to the experience and continue to feel them over and over. All of this leads us to the bigger *why: why* is this coming up in our life? That bigger why can help us find some level of peace, even in the hardest moments. That doesn't mean we bypass our experience here on earth, but it does allow us to put our experience into its greater context.

And that, my friends, is the final piece of the puzzle. When things finally click into place, it's life-changing, because it allows us to heal parts of ourselves that we actually incarnated in order to heal. That's when we are able to change the frequency of our behavior and do things differently. Even just recognizing the presence of a life lesson and working to explore it makes this shift possible.

If none of this is sinking in for you right now, don't worry—you don't have to seek out your life lessons; they will surely find you in your own time. And if you're deep in it right now and can't figure out what's being triggered, that's OK, too, because the lessons will come. You are bound to start processing the items in your shopping cart, and your Guides are at your side to make sense of it when you do.

If, on the other hand, you are able to see and make sense of some life lessons at this moment, you may find that the process brings some relief from your worldly woes. Seeing with this perspective won't make things easy—life lessons are difficult by their very nature. Instead, it offers us a way to work through the challenges of our lives—big and small—on a spiritual level, as well as a physical, earthly level.

Eventually, we'll be able to see through the material world to the life lessons underneath even more quickly. We'll be able to discern what is and is not ours to work on, and we'll be able to do that work in a more focused way, without the ego's distractions. We'll reach gratitude more quickly, even when we're smack-dab in the middle of something difficult. Something that once would take us months or years to process can be resolved in a matter of weeks, days, or sometimes even hours. That's when we know we are close to breaking the cycle by comprehending what our soul yearns for us to understand.

Soul Contracts

Working with a particular lesson over and over makes us much more efficient at seeing beyond the veil of illusion and understanding what is happening on a spiritual level. Eventually, we crack the code and break through to a new plane. This is how we complete our soul contracts.

Of course, the idea that everything is happening on a spiritual level does not save us from the pain of having it happen on the physical plane. It's not as simple as saying that our souls signed up for these lessons and leaving it at that. Part of our work is to understand the spiritual level without compromising the compassion we have for what is happening in our physical reality. That includes compassion for ourselves and compassion for others.

Sometimes our life lesson is to accept that what is happening may not feel spiritual at all—it's beyond meaning or reason entirely. In those circumstances we have to just feel all our feelings, without bypassing them, knowing we are each entitled to our experience.

Aimee, the friend I wrote about in chapter 7, is attracted to chaotic life changes. She bounces from psychic to psychic trying to make sense of *why* instability calls to her. She has become completely lost in the spiritual side of life and has neglected the physical side. Aimee is undoubtedly working with a soul contract—the same lesson has come to her too many times, and in too many ways, for it to be anything but that. However, Aimee has become lost by thinking that the work she has to do is solely on the spiritual level. The physical level is in fact the only place where she can make a change.

In the same way, though I understand my work with imposter syndrome and comparison is a major lesson my soul came here to work with, and though that knowing alone is very powerful, it isn't the entirety of the work I have to do. I have to allow gratitude when I feel envy; I have to take my seat at the table even when I feel I am not enough; and I have to see the best in everyone around me.

The way we know we are complete with a soul contract is when an event comes along that would otherwise send us spinning right off the road, but somehow, this time, it doesn't.

Earlier this summer, just before I began writing this book, I had a dream about a bunch of tornadoes hitting Florida. We had just started the build on our new house there, and so I passed the dream off as me just being nervous about living in a new place. But long after the dream the image just kept coming back to me: a dark, menacing twister skating down the street in our new housing development, tearing down everything in its path. I started to develop a tornado in my stomach, which intensified when we took a trip down to our rented Florida condo to check up on the building process.

I was antsy, jumpy, and when there were storms, I kept looking over my shoulder in anticipation of the tornado from my imagination manifesting in real time.

But no tornadoes came. Throughout the fall, as I got deeper into the writing process with this book, I found myself with opportunities to work on my other issues and kind of forgot about my strange tornado fantasy.

Then came Hurricane Milton.

The morning after the hurricane I turned on the news in our Long Island rental house while my husband and I made the morning coffee. The anchor told of the destruction throughout Florida, explaining how people had lost their homes and, in some cases, even their lives. Then as a field reporter started speaking, the broadcast showed still images from around the region. One was an image of a dumpster on a roof. "Oh, those poor people," I started to say to my husband, but stopped short as we both had the same realization at the exact same time: that the street looked familiar.

Really familiar, in fact.

It was our street.

The next hours were a blur. We quickly determined that our home-in-progress had indeed been hit by a tornado. While we were financially protected, this would set the building process back significantly.

I was, and am, grateful that my family is OK, my immediate neighbors are OK, and that my husband and I were not in our new home yet. Instead of panicking about what we had lost—or more significantly in my process, how it affected my fears about safety and stability—I could lean into a sense of joyful detachment. "It's just a house," I kept saying, and I meant it.

Many people lost their homes in this hurricane, and for many of them, their loss isn't just a house—it's devastating. I don't want my experience to diminish theirs in any way. I am aware that our home wasn't complete, that we have other places to live, that we have not lost family members or been financially destroyed by this event. That surely makes it easier. But still, a few months ago and certainly years ago, I would have been consumed with my own process around it. It would have brought up so much insecurity, and I would have started questioning all the decisions that led up to that moment. At my worst, I may have even entered into a story in my mind about losing my sense of security—even though we hadn't moved in yet.

Instead, within minutes of hearing this news that directly hits my life lesson around stability and a sense of home, I managed to arrive in a space of gratitude, focusing instead on what I still have. I know it's just a house; it's shelter, and we will build it again.

In large part, I can attribute this shift in perspective to the security and comfort I feel in my family today—the opposite of what I experienced when I dreamed about drowning in my father's Buick. My husband and I have known each other since we were kids, but it was my Guides who called me into a relationship with him in my forties. *There he is, that's the one,* I remember thinking. At that point in my life, I was beginning to actively understand my soul contract with people-pleasing, and aside from my children (who adored him), I didn't care what anyone thought from the outside because I knew he was right for me.

In the years our relationship has developed, I've stepped into who I am as a human being. I've claimed my truth as a psychic medium, which my husband fully supports even though it's entirely uncommon in our social circles and makes me stick out a bit. He has become my home and my grounding, and the life we've built together has transformed many of the insecurities I felt early in life into challenges I have the fortitude to confront. He didn't make my life perfect—no person can do that for another person—but he was crucial in helping to build the foundation of my happiness today. Our family structure has become my home. As a result, I'm just not that attached to any building.

My concerns are no longer about whether I'm OK because my inner sense of security is untouched. My worst-case scenario has taken place, and somehow, it just isn't that big of a deal, because I have found an unshakable sense of home in the world. Within an hour of seeing the news about Hurricane Milton, my husband and I quickly discussed what we needed to do and got to work: making the phone calls, signing the papers, and rebuilding what the tornado had destroyed.

When I related this to a friend of mine, she suggested that perhaps this was a sign we weren't meant to move to Florida. For someone else, or for me on another timeline, perhaps it would be. But my Guides are clear that this is not the case this time around. It's just a random thing that happened, which gave me the opportunity to practice my life lesson around the sense of inner security my soul came here to experience. Deep down, I know this to be true.

I don't have exclusive access to this knowing because I am a psychic medium. We all have it. You are the only one who can truly understand the meaning of the events in your life and how they relate to the lessons you incarnated to learn. Some events have little meaning, while others are much more significant; some are easier to work through, while others take decades or may not be fully resolved this time around. Our Guides show us the way through our inner knowing.

There is such relief in reaching the end of a soul contract. I can see the hard work that led me here and be grateful for it. I can appreciate even the most difficult parts of the journey, seeing the light and grace that carried me through them. I can look back and understand how it all fits together, how absolutely no other set of events could have brought me where I am today, and I can feel proud of myself for weathering it all as best I could—at times adeptly, at other times awkwardly.

I wish for you this same feeling. I know it is possible, because nearly everyone finishes at least one soul contract in each lifetime. For some, this will be a purely light and joyful process all the way through. For most of us it will be tougher, and for some it will be truly heart-wrenching. We aren't all given the same route to follow. Some people have come here with especially tough lessons to learn, and all we can do is hope that they have moments of clarity that bring them some peace in parts of their life anyway. At some point, we will all break through and finish the contract—whether it's in this lifetime or another. And then, freedom awaits.

While you're on your way, it can be helpful to get a little more clarity about what you came here to work on. The following exercise will help.

EXERCISE: WHAT'S IN YOUR CART?

This exercise, inspired by Betty Guadagno's experience, involves visualizing a common scenario for many of us: online shopping! It may help to set the scene with some repetitive music or by lighting a candle. Then cleanse and ground yourself. Take a moment to thank your highest self for what it is about to show you.

Start with something that is really challenging for you at the moment—a life lesson you feel certain you came here to work with. Envision scenes in your life in which you encountered it; let each one play out, and then move to the next.

For instance, perhaps you have been working with body image. See an early experience during which you were shamed for your body by a family member. Then see yourself as a pubescent teen, hiding your body from your peers. See yourself again in an early relationship, then later in life. Run through the instances in your mind. Really feel the depth of this life lesson.

Then, connect with your highest being and watch yourself choose it. Click on it and add it to your cart. Allow your highest knowing to accept that you chose this, for whatever reason, and that your soul is committed to learning it in its entirety.

Allow your mind to move on to something else that nags at you. Let it call you, and start to watch the scenes play out as the life lesson reveals itself. You may be familiar with this theme or it may be presenting itself to you for the first time. Once you've seen the essence of the lesson through numerous scenes and you feel ready, imagine yourself clicking on it and adding it to your cart. You may even repeat a phrase to yourself like, "I chose this," or "Added to cart."

Do this three more times, for a total of five lessons.

Then, see yourself clicking on "View cart," and look at your five lessons all together. Can you truly believe you chose them? Can you be that honest with yourself? A little resistance is a good thing here, because it means you've really picked your life lessons. Sit with your feelings without judgment.

Now it's time to call your Guides into the process. You can call a particular Guide if you have one in mind or just your Guides more generally. This can be formal or informal—by this point in the process, you'll know the communication style that works best for you.

When your Guides arrive, ask whether they have any wisdom to impart about these lessons. The lessons may be connected, for instance, or your Guides may have thoughts on how you can finish the soul contract with one or more of them if you are close to doing so. They may advise you to focus on one lesson above the others right now or to surrender fighting a particular lesson that is hard for you to accept. Hear what they have to say with love and appreciation.

Then thank your Guides for what they have told you, and when you are complete with the exercise, thank yourself. Be sure to journal, practice automatic writing, or otherwise record some of this powerful experience to reflect upon later.

Chapter 11
TAKE THE WHEEL

UP TO THIS POINT, WE'VE BEEN WORKING ON GIVING OUR GUIDES more and more power in our lives. We've been practicing shutting down the mind, harnessing the ego, and letting our Guides lead us. If you've used the exercises I've provided, integrating them into your life as you see fit, you've done the work in that regard. You've made good progress!

There's an important difference, however, between giving our Guides power and giving our power over to them. Our Guides understand this distinction well and want to lead us to our own comprehension of it. There's a reason they're sitting in the passenger's seat, not driving the car. What they want—what all the Universe wants for us, in fact—is for us to take the wheel.

The most important thing I want you to learn from this entire book is housed within this chapter: the idea that our active, joyful participation in our lives—spiritual and physical, wooey and practical—is essential. It's what's intended for us. It's the entire point of coming to this plane actually. We're meant to steer our lives, with a balanced combination of divine guidance and free will.

We're meant to steer our lives, with a balanced combination of divine guidance and free will.

In the book I wrote before this one, *Medium Mentor*, I advocated for designing your own spiritual practice. Here I'm taking that idea a step further. I suggest you design not only your own spiritual practice but also your entire life. Where do you want to go—literally and figuratively? What people do you want to be with? What do you want to do? What matters most to you? Which hearts do you want to touch? What kind of world do you want to create? What do you want to leave behind when you depart? This isn't a mental exercise; living the answers to these questions is an ongoing process that evolves in every moment, building that twisting, turning road as we travel it.

This shift toward becoming the driver of our own lives has three main steps. First, we have to release the details of what we *think* our inner spiritual life, our exterior life, and our practice should look like so we can use our claircognizance to *feel* what is right for us. Then, from that place, we can manifest what we want. Once we have the main elements in place, we can continue forward while checking in with our Guides along the way, making a daily habit of asking them to lead us toward the decisions that will be best for us. This doesn't absolve us of doing the work—in fact, our Guides will sometimes ask us to work really hard! Instead, it means we won't act blindly or alone. With our Guides in the passenger seat, we will have all the support we need to make our moves.

Release the Details

It's time for me to share with you one of the highest-level spiritual truths I know:

> *Spirit doesn't care what you call the power you believe in.*
>
> *Spirit doesn't need you to go through any ritual or keep to any practice.*
>
> *Spirit doesn't care what words you use or what songs you sing. Spirit doesn't care about your crystals or your decks, or value one over the other. None of those things are the point.*
>
> *They're all just tools to get you to do one thing: to feel connected to Spirit, completely connected, as if you are one. This connection is the only thing that matters. It is queen over all other things. Everything else is just a detail.*

That can be a little bit scary to realize, because it means that there's no set of things anyone can do, say, or believe that is going to expedite the shifts they want to make in their life. Instead, we have to *truly feel* our connection to

Spirit, Source, and self, and *act* from that place. No one is coming to save us. There is no magic button or Magic 8 Ball. It's all on us.

At the same time, it's incredibly freeing to realize this is the case. With each breath we can connect inward. With each action and statement we can hold true to what the Universe intends for us. On the one hand, it's just that simple—*eek, how scary!* On the other, it's just that simple—*whew, how easy!*

That's why other teachers working with the law of attraction, manifestation, and the like want us to focus so hard on feeling like we already have what we want to attract. It's the same reason thought leaders connecting spirituality and neuroscience go to such great lengths to show us how our thoughts create our reality. Dr. James Doty at Stanford University School of Medicine's Center for Compassion and Altruism Research and Education (CCARE) coined the term *embedding your intention*, which explains how a positive focus can train our brain to create a positive reality. Once it is attuned to the positive, the brain will go to great lengths to seek out more positivity. Manifestation therefore has a neurological basis, because our perception helps us create the world we live in. From a spiritual perspective, this means that we are co-creating right alongside Spirit.

As co-creators of the Universe, our inner experience has tremendous power over our external circumstances. No, our inner experience isn't the only factor—I'm not trying to gaslight you about the sometimes unfortunate realities of this world and the many external pressures and systems that hold people back. But our inner experience plays an essential role in our physical understanding of the world. Our belief is a crucial piece of the puzzle. And since it's the only one we can really, truly control, it's the one most worthy of our attention.

When we shift our perspective and become curious about why, on the higher level, we are faced with the challenges that come our way, we move ourselves out of fear and reactivity and into trust instead. This raises our vibration significantly and brings more of what we want to us. Using positive affirmation and clear intention about our thought process, we start to see the world with a different lens, transforming obstacles into opportunities for whatever our soul needs next. Sometimes what our soul needs is the exact opposite of what our ego wants. When we defer to that higher understanding, we start to co-create new timelines.

My friend, actor and presenter Maria Menounos, calls this "choosing wonder over worry." She has experienced a really difficult set of challenges in life, and when I met her, she was recovering from surgery for a brain tumor. It was sometime after that her mother died, which put Maria into a deep grief she had never known before. Meanwhile, she was manifesting becoming a mother, something that was difficult after these challenges.

Maria's guidance pushed her to take real-world steps, and eventually she opted to have a baby via a surrogate. During the pregnancy, she was diagnosed with pancreatic cancer. One of the things that allowed her to persevere was the belief that there was a bigger lesson for her in all of it. Instead of worrying about things she couldn't control on this plane, she focused on wondering what that lesson was and how she could learn it more fully. Maria maintained her focus and now is blessed with her beautiful daughter Athena.

Choosing wonder over worry helped Maria access that higher mindset even when things were unbelievably difficult for her. That gave her Guides space to show her what decisions to make to move forward. Had she just stayed in fear or self-pity, she couldn't have gotten there.

When things become difficult for me, I get to writing things down. I roll with a pen and a notebook almost everywhere I go. I make lists, write affirmations, and scribble away in my notebook. Others may look at me and think I'm a peaceful, happy little journaler, but the truth is that the busier my pages become, the more likely I'm struggling inside. I take that struggle as an opportunity to get to work in the spiritual realm.

My mind can stay busy, but my hand can only write one thing at a time. Writing forces me to choose a dominant thought, and I am determined to make that thought positive! So when I'm stressed about my body, I choose, ***My body is strong***; when I'm worried about financial matters, I choose, ***Money is flowing***; when I'm impatient about my housing situation, I choose, ***I love my home***. This, combined with my focus on wonder about the higher lessons at play, shifts me out of fear and into the positive space where manifestation is possible.

In the last few years, my notebooks have been pretty packed. It hasn't been comfortable, but I refuse to let fear overwhelm me, so I just let my pen fly! I was therefore a little bit nervous when my Guides told me it was time to write this book. *Really?! Now?!* I knew that there was no way I could do it without exposing myself during a vulnerable time, and that thought wasn't exactly comfortable! But I knew I had to do it anyway. If I am being guided to write during such a raw phase of my life, exposing that rawness must be part of the lesson for me.

When our Guides make concrete requests, they're showing us the real-world steps we have to take. That's right—manifesting is more than just calling things into existence. It takes real effort and concrete actions.

What Manifesting Isn't

There's more to manifesting than directing the vectors of our attention. We must also direct our action and make intentional moves to enact the change we wish to see.

Manifesting isn't just putting in our order and sitting around waiting for things to happen. There are nearly always real-life moves for us to make—often, ones that challenge us and push us out of our comfort zone. Part of our Guides' role is to show us what those actions are. We have to be willing to invest our time and energy into bringing our manifestation to fruition.

Much of this work involves removing the obstacles that prevent our manifestation from taking place. That could be clearing out thoughts from our mental sphere, but it could also involve clearing away people, places, things, or activities. Can we be brave enough to walk away from something that isn't serving us without a good reason, but simply because we know it to be true? Can we let go of what everyone else thinks? Can we make our moves based on what is authentic in Spirit, regardless of whether they make logical sense to us in the moment?

One of my students, Christine, has taken seven years to transition from her career as an attorney to working as a psychic full-time. Christine has created vision boards, posted affirmations all over her house, and spoken her psychic career into reality. But among the vision boards and positive affirmations about her psychic career, Christine has also taken classes and workshops, signed up for a one-on-one mentorship program with me, and read for hundreds of other students. She's worked to create solid boundaries around her psychic mediumship practice, first doing them in the evenings while running her law practice in the daytime, then cutting back from her law practice slowly while her psychic income increased.

Christine has also had to make relationship changes. As you can likely imagine, not everyone in her social sphere was open to her psychic work. She has strengthened supportive friendships while letting unsupportive ones cool. In some cases, she has remained close friends with people who didn't understand her career shift, but created boundaries around what she shares with them and what she doesn't, just as she has done with unsupportive members of her family. All of these moves came from the guidance she received along the way, and they are just as important as the mental shifts she made.

To do these things, Christine had to trust in herself and her guidance. She also had to trust in divine timing, knowing that things were unfolding exactly as they needed to unfold. By the time she was financially ready to begin working as a psychic full-time, her thoughts had prepared her to do so, and her actions had prepared her life to embrace her new career path. She was surrounded by supportive people and was already living a lifestyle that allowed for the seamless integration of her new workload. For Christine, slow and steady was the method that helped her manifest her dream.

Like I wrote in ***Believe, Ask, Act***, manifesting isn't just sitting on our meditation cushion and waiting for things to happen. It requires real-world steps like the ones Christine made. It also requires us to trust when things ***don't*** work out—or don't work out immediately, at least. Gabby Bernstein, my dear friend, is such a great example of this. She's the best manifestor I have ever met! Whether it's a dinner reservation or a successful best-selling book, Gabby sets the intention and speaks it into existence. She is one of the hardest-working people I know, and isn't afraid to take steps toward manifesting what she wants.

But Gabby also applies an extra level to her method of manifestation: she really, truly accepts when things don't come to fruition, integrating this into her understanding of what's "meant to be." While she holds true to her vision, she releases her ego and expectation, getting that when things don't manifest there's something for her there, too. "All right, clearly I'm being protected," I've heard her say. "Let me see what else I'm receiving instead."

That's right: rejection is protection! My friend Joanie had a firsthand experience of this recently. She was being pushed to do more and more at her corporate job, where her workload seemed to increase with each cut at the company. It didn't make sense: though she was helping her company earn more each year, her superiors kept cutting the budget, resulting in layoffs that kept Joanie at her desk after hours. She shared with me what was going on as her friend. I told her she had to push for better treatment, which she assured me aligned with the guidance she was receiving from her Universal Team. But her conversations with her manager, and eventually her manager's manager, were fruitless. She just couldn't get the respect she deserved at her workplace, even after almost a decade of service, and it hurt.

The next time we met, Joanie told me how she'd been turned down. "Why don't you leave?" I suggested. "It doesn't sound like they deserve you, and you're super-valuable. You'll find another job quickly, I think." Joanie deflected, citing a competitive job market and her hope that things would get better. Though I was worried for her, I dropped it, knowing her Guides would show her the way.

Then Joanie called me with the worst news: she'd been offered a choice between taking on more work or accepting a layoff. Frustrated with the situation, Joanie had opted to leave. She had been given an hour to pack up her desk and wipe her computer, and then she was escorted to the elevator by a security guard. "I'm crushed," she said, tearing up. "I did everything I could. I just couldn't give them any more." I listened with an open heart, trying to be there for my friend.

As she talked, she went from sadness to anger. "I can't believe they would do this to me! How stupid can they be? They're losing all their best employees!" I kept listening, holding the space.

Then Joanie shifted again. This time, she sounded almost elated. "I don't know, I feel so done with that place. I can't believe I spent so many years there. I feel . . . I guess . . . relieved! Like I'm finally free!"

This is when I stepped in to share what I was seeing in the situation. I told Joanie that her Guides had heard what she needed, even when her manager hadn't. They were freeing her up for something better to come along. Each time she asked for a fair workload and received pushback, she was getting closer to freedom. And her Guides wanted her to design her new, ideal career move—one that would fit in with the rest of her life.

It didn't take long. That weekend, Joanie went to a retreat and explained what had happened onstage. She got vulnerable, telling the group how much she wanted to work doing what she loved. At the next break another audience member approached her to say their company was hiring! Joanie is now happy at her new position where her needs are respected and her contribution is valued.

Our Guides can tell us when we need to keep pushing for what we want, whether it's through shifting our mindset or making steps in our lives, and when we need to release what we think is best for us in order to understand the higher plan in play. Truly taking the wheel requires us to trust this discernment.

If you're pushing for something that just doesn't seem to be happening right now, ask your Guides: *What am I not seeing here?* Like Joanie, they may be telling you it's time to make a drastic change yourself. Or they may show you the work you've been avoiding. They may indicate a thought you need to push past and replace with something more positive. And they may show you that, though you want something, it isn't for you. Perhaps it isn't what you need right now or it isn't for you in the way that you thought. If that's the case, the action you may need to take is to shift your goal just slightly.

Again, no one can do this for you. No psychic can tell you what's right. This work is all internal—it's all you. And that means you need to be strong enough and brave enough to look at the situation honestly and trust the guidance you receive. The inner knowing is within you—deep down, you get your story. The role of Guides is to point you to it so you can remember the answers that lie dormant, waiting for you.

If you look closely, you'll see that we've been discussing these ideas throughout the book—roadblocks, traffic jams, detours, and the like. Yet it's often hard to identify just what's happening in our own lives—are we meant to pause, create a new route, or something else? Many of my students and nearly all of my clients come to me hoping I can do this for them. But the biggest and most important job we have on our spiritual journey is learning to do this for ourselves. This discernment is tricky. It's personal. It's delicate. It requires trial and error, as we celebrate our wins and forgive ourselves for our mistakes.

And that isn't *in opposition* to the rest of our spiritual work—it's *part of it*. As co-creators, our very manifestation is based on our ability to discern. We're not supposed to know how to do it very well; we're supposed to learn as we go.

The more you clear your channel, the more this discernment is possible. That's why I encourage you to keep an open conversation going with your Guides, checking in with them so often that it becomes second nature.

Make Asking a Habit

In my day-to-day life, I am in constant conversation with my Guides.

We have a very deep and personal relationship. It's so personal, in fact, that they often take on my own intuitive voice. They're the first to pipe up when a question arises, providing an initial reaction I can trust.

Our Guides come through that very first reaction. Now, I'm not referring to the mind's ongoing excuse or explanation—anything drawn out or detailed comes from the mental sphere, not that guidance. Instead, I'm referring to that knee-jerk yes or no that many people attribute to the gut.

If you've ever seen someone who works with muscle testing, you may have noticed how they'll just feel the answer in their body in a split second. These people are often excellent healers and intuitives, because they have tuned their body to that initial response and know how to trust it. Because their bodies have become such effective tools for them, they check in with them dozens of times each day, and they follow the response they receive.

We can all learn to do this—whether it's through muscle testing our body or just through listening to that yes or no that comes up. The more we practice it, the better we get at it.

Trusting the answer we receive is a key component of the process of spiritual discernment. It's one I really had to work to understand. Many times I've pushed through a no I've received—to read for someone, to weigh in on something—with disastrous results. I've learned to not do this anymore and have become quite proficient at listening to a no, even when it's uncomfortable or doesn't make logical sense.

Other times, I'm able to successfully negotiate with my Guides. *You've had enough. Take a break!* they'll say. "Look, I have a workshop scheduled and a couple of media appearances that I can't cancel. Can you give me two more weeks, until the 15th? Then I promise to take a break!" I'll respond. ***OK, but cancel everything you can between now and then, and be vigilant about your self-care,*** I'll hear back, and when I do that (and when I actually keep my schedule calm after the 15th, holding to my side of the bargain), they'll usually support me. This sort of back-and-forth makes it possible for me to ask for guidance regularly, even when I'm worried about what I'll hear in response.

Fostering a continued, ongoing dialogue with our Guides helps us co-create our reality. It helps us manifest what we want our lives to look and feel like. It also brings us to a higher vibration—one that can assist us in manifesting beyond our wildest dreams. Just by bringing our Guides into our daily, hourly, even minute-to-minute awareness, we raise ourselves up, elevating ourselves to attune with the highest and best.

Doing so reminds us that no matter how dire our circumstances may seem in the moment, however far we may feel from what we want, the light we are seeking is *right here*. It's millimeters from our fingertips. I can't tell you how many clients and students I've worked with over the years who are trying to free themselves from something—some pattern repeating throughout the generations of their family or within their romantic or platonic relationships or their connection to money or home or work or a health challenge or an experience they can't get past. Again and again they ask me: "How do I elevate myself out of this, not only personally, but spiritually?"

The answer is always the same: reach for the guidance that is available to you. Your situation may or may not immediately improve—I make no promises on that—but your perspective will flip around in a second. And it is that new perspective that will bring you more of what you want, guaranteed.

Asking is a habit for me whenever I feel myself start to lock up. My Guides answer me in such wild ways. The day after my friend Diana died, I was sitting with Phoenix and everything felt so difficult. So I asked. "Help; show me something; give me a sign that it's going to be OK," I pleaded with my Guides. I couldn't even really focus on what I was asking, though, because Phoenix started whining to go outside.

I went to the door and opened it, my mind still half focused on my unfinished prayer. Phoenix, who generally just wanders out on his own, took a few steps and then stopped to look at me. It's as if he were saying, *Come on. I need you to join me.*

So I decided to keep asking on the go. I slipped on some shoes and followed him out. It was a beautiful sunny day, with wispy white clouds adding gentle texture to an otherwise perfectly blue sky. There wasn't a rain cloud in sight, which was a bit disappointing because Diana often communicates through rainbows. Phoenix wandered around sniffing things—truly, isn't this the best activity for elder dogs?—and I continued to focus on Diana, asking for a greater understanding to put context to my grief. She was only forty. She left behind a wonderful husband. Though as a psychic medium she understood death on a deep and personal level, she hadn't wanted to die, and her passing felt so tragic. How could I make sense of it? Phoenix sniffed the leg of the outdoor dining table, then a patio chair. I followed him with my gaze.

Sit, I heard Spirit's voice say loud and clear, just as my eyes landed on the chair. I studied the chair. I didn't ask questions; I sat.

Look up.

There, I saw a rainbow glittering among the clouds. It wasn't an arc reaching up from the horizon, but more like a smear of multicolored light streaming down from above. Across it moved a wisp of cotton cloud in the shape of an angel.

"Diana, you show-off," I whispered. I recorded it on my phone and sent it to our mutual friends as well as her husband, since we were all missing Diana so much.

When we ask, we receive. When we make that asking a habit, we become a channel for guidance. It's just that simple.

So how can we make the jump from targeted spiritual practice, from moments of manifestation, to an automatic, ongoing, co-created spiritual life that is integrated into our every moment?

It comes down to a choice to perceive things through a new perspective—to shift our inner dialogue so we can speak the world we want into existence. We are remarkably powerful beings. It's really up to us to heal.

When we ask, we call in the light. We welcome Spirit into our lives, whatever shape they may be in within that moment, and immediately we are elevated. We take responsibility, understanding that we came here with these lessons and it's up to us to get to work figuring them out.

This is how we take complete accountability for our lives. We accept that we are responsible, not for everything that happens to us, but for what we make of it. That means if something great happens, we integrate it; if something terrible happens, we either find a way to spin it positively or to make meaning of the fact that we *can't* do that. We show up with our authentic selves—all our emotion, all our hopes and desires, and zero apologies. We accept ourselves and our world entirely, whatever is happening, in every moment. We use it to co-create the next moment, and the one after that, however we see fit.

We take the wheel of our lives, and by doing so, we embrace the reason for our incarnation.

EXERCISE: MANIFESTING MEDITATION

For this meditation, you'll need a pen and paper.

First, cleanse and ground yourself.

Then focus on something you've been thinking about lately. It could be an upcoming vacation, a job change, a friendship—anything really! Just choose something that has been on your mind.

Write down what you want, or what you think you want if you're unclear. What do you want to have happen? Who might be involved? Where might this take place? Feel free to write as many things as feel true to you, and don't worry about whether they seem possible in this moment or even if they contradict each other. Just let your pen flow.

Next close your notebook and put your pen down. Make yourself comfortable to meditate.

Take a few deep breaths and close your eyes. Then focus on a place where you like to meet your Guides. You may have found such a place before; it may be a spot in nature, like a forest clearing or a beach. It may be a temple or other structure you have conjured in the past when connecting with your Guides. Call a Guide or several Guides in to join you.

When you feel them arrive, ask for their input. What do they see for you? What will be best for you? You may be surprised to notice the similarities and differences from what you wrote down.

Thank them and close your meditation however works for you. (You may choose to back away slowly in your mind's eye, bow yourself down to the floor, etc.)

Open your eyes and pick up your pen again. Write what your Guides showed or told you. Then compare it to what you wrote before the meditation and see if there's a difference. Don't worry about making sense of what you'll do right now—that will come. For now, just notice how you and your Guides are co-creating together.

Over the next few days, you will receive breadcrumbs on the path toward this vision you and your Guides developed. It is imperative that you recognize and go where they lead, even if they don't make sense. Practice this and you will see that when you follow the signs and opportunities that present themselves, you are taking the path your Guides have laid for you.

[illegible]

[illegible] and the work they were to do with [illegible]

[illegible] may have a [illegible] that [illegible] Mother Mary. This parish may see Mary who [illegible]

Chapter 12
"YOU HAVE ARRIVED"—OR HAVE YOU?

A FUNNY THING HAPPENS WHEN WE ACCEPT THE TASK OF LIVING authentically, taking accountability for our lives. We gain confidence. We learn that, even when we make mistakes, we are guided. We give up our fear of detours and embrace the long road. We start to trust in ourselves and the Universe.

We start to own what we've chosen and the route we've taken. When we look back and see what we've overcome, we feel a sense of pride. We realize: ***Hey, I really like myself! And I like being alive, too!*** Even in the hardest moments when we're facing big challenges, we have a glimmer of hope. We receive grace.

We start to speak self-confidence right down into our core. We celebrate our accomplishments loudly and proudly, and we champion the accomplishments of others, becoming unabashed cheerleaders of life. We develop value, love, and validation for ourselves, and we think positively of the world around us. Doing so heals old wounds from way back when. It brings good experiences our way by helping us find the positive in what comes. It makes us a beacon of support for those around us, who want to support us in turn.

We stop looking for the end of the road, because we realize we really, truly enjoy the process of getting there. There is no more daily grind: instead, there's just daily adventure.

We see this life in its greater context as a soul's journey, and everything transforms.

It Never Ends

When all is said and done, we will start all over again. This road never ends. At some point we realize that "you have arrived" doesn't refer to a location, it refers to a perspective: one that embraces the fact that there is no "there" to get to.

Even once we reach this perspective, we're likely to forget it again. This is part of the process, too. Over time, however, we start to find our perspective more quickly.

I still fall into fear frequently. When one of my open soul contracts arrives, it's easy for me to slam on the brakes in panic. In chapter 5, I told you about the world's most uncomfortable dinner. A decade ago, I would have stayed in my discomfort for weeks or months before sitting down with a journal and a meditation cushion to hash it out. Nowadays, it often only takes me an hour. I feel myself getting riled up and hear my mental chatter start to get faster and faster, and I know I have to get to work.

The ego will come up with a million reasons why we ***shouldn't*** do the work. This doesn't change, it just gets easier to recognize. ***It's not me; it's the situation!*** it will whine. ***I'll work on myself with another issue . . . I promise. Just not this one,*** it explains.

In fact, the more it explains, the more we can know what we're hearing is the ego. As I shared in chapter 7, true guidance is short and sweet. ***Not my issue,*** it'll say—and that's it. No elaboration.

As soon as we hear the train of excuses, one piling up on top of the other, we can be sure it's the ego trying to avoid doing its work. That is an ongoing process even the most spiritually enlightened people face. All we can do is keep showing up again and again, working on ourselves the best we can. Our Guides will always support us in this endeavor.

And as you've heard before, it's often darkest right before the dawn. As we reach the end of a soul contract, things come to a kind of crescendo. We get the lightning round, the grand finale, challenges popping up left and right to see if we really, truly get it yet. This is how we know we're nearing the end with a particular issue.

Celeste attended one of my workshops just a few months after the unexpected passing of her husband, Brent. He died of a massive heart attack at the age of fifty-one. In the first few exercises of the workshop, Celeste appeared somewhat timid, unsure of what she wanted. It was clear she was still reeling from his loss and was trying to make sense of who she is without her partner.

When we did a past-life meditation, Brent showed himself to Celeste. He first confirmed for her, as many loved ones do, that he was OK on the Other Side and had a strong sense of why he had passed so suddenly. They shared some loving moments together, remembering the marriage they had spent two decades building. He then shifted his face to show her what he had looked like in a past life.

In this lifetime, Celeste understood, they were also a married couple. It was some time around the Industrial Revolution, based on the imagery Celeste described, and he had been killed suddenly while working in a factory. It was a time when being a widow was very difficult socially; women didn't have a lot of job options, and finding her place in society was difficult for Celeste. Brent told her that because she hadn't fully learned her lesson around how to exist without a partner that time around, they'd repeated the same events again. She now has another opportunity to learn it, this time in a more forgiving social atmosphere that offers more space for her to be who she is.

Celeste realized that in many areas of her life—professional, social, and now as a single woman—she was being asked to step into her authenticity and show up as her whole self with no apologies. She was being asked to identify what she liked and what she wanted, and then to go out and get it. Attending the workshop that weekend was a part of this process for her. If she chose, Brent assured her through the past-life meditation, she could learn the lesson in full and end her soul contract. She'd have to give up her habit of playing small and deferring to other people's desires; she'd have to stop people-pleasing. In return, she'd be set free. The choice was up to her.

Many of us have at least one area of our life in which we are being offered a similar choice to end a soul contract. I know this is the case for many of the struggles I've shared with you throughout these pages. At this point I'd say my habits of comparison and competition are on their way out. They're cropping up so often and I'm catching them so fast that I really know something is happening. But I recognize that even when that contract finishes, I'll just move on to a deeper one. This is how we grow. It's part of the human experience.

That's right—there is no conclusion that says "I'm done" or "I have it all figured out." I'm not, and I don't. None of us are done. None of us has it figured out. We're all in this together, doing the best we can.

In fact, the minute any of us thinks we're done, we should try to write a book about it. ***Are you sure?*** our Guides will ask, teasing us gently. ***Do you really get it? Are you really ready to put this down?*** That's when the tests get even more raw and even more real.

Passing Familiar Landmarks

As I explained in chapter 10, soul contracts are completed when we are presented with a situation that would previously be deeply upsetting to us, but we stay grounded and centered instead.

In the lead-up to this experience, we are hyperaware that the Universe is messing with us. As we pass familiar landmarks again and again, we start to relate to them differently. We begin to connect past events to what is happening today and understand why these seemingly small events threaten to send us spinning in 360s. We find ways to make peace with our past, accepting fully what happened (regardless of whether or not we approve of it), and truly wish for things to be different going forward. We are deeply committed to do what it takes to make that happen.

Sometimes a memory or phrase will start repeating in our head—similar to my experience with "Cora Street," which I told you about in chapter 6. I call this experience *memory planting*. This is when, even without us asking, the origin of our challenge in this lifetime tries to reveal itself to us.

For instance, as I come toward the end of my contract with impostor syndrome, I keep thinking back to my eighth grade student council election.

In the eighth grade, I was the student council secretary. My parents were in the middle of their divorce, and the position helped stabilize me during a tumultuous time. I was missing school a lot because I just wanted to sit alone and cry. I wasn't a star student that year, but I took being secretary seriously.

Then I ran for student council president, and I won! I was surprised and so excited. The win gave me something to feel good about, and I was looking forward to giving it my all the following year.

Almost immediately, I was called into a one-on-one meeting with one of my teachers. She broke the news to me that I couldn't be the president because I'd missed so much school as the secretary. Popular vote was one thing, she indicated, but this position was something for serious students others could emulate—in other words, ***not me***. Word spread like wildfire around the student body. The whole school knew I won, and then the whole school knew that the administration had taken the win away from me because I wasn't good enough.

Over the last few months, this memory has nagged at me. It came up while I was driving, and in the checkout line at the grocery store, and again on a walk. It was just a passing thought, so I didn't take it very seriously, but then I recognized I was being shown something. Finally, I asked my Guides, "What is this about? What do I need to see here?"

You deserve success, I heard in response. ***You are good enough. Nothing is going to be taken away from you.***

I realized that every time I experience success, I'm waiting for the other shoe to drop. I'm waiting to learn that I'm a fraud or that I don't deserve whatever it is I've worked so hard to get.

Looking back on that memory from the 1980s, I barely even understand it. How could no one check in with me when I started missing so much school? It was completely out of the blue—not at all my norm. How could it be that no teacher or administrator said, "Hey MaryAnn, what's going on in your life? Why are you skipping school so much?" Instead, they assumed I was a bad kid, and the rest of the students wanting me to be student body president couldn't dissuade them.

When our Guides start showing us a memory like this, they're trying to free us from something that has been plaguing us for a long time. They're helping us link the familiar landmarks together, showing us the pattern, because the emotional experiences we didn't fully process in the past are the ones we are destined to experience again.

This is true of all the experiences in this lifetime, and sometimes even of experiences from past lifetimes. I recently read for a woman at an event where it was clear to me that she had fought at Gettysburg in the Civil War. I blurted this out rather unceremoniously, because it came to me all of a sudden, and her jaw dropped. "I can't believe you're saying that! I can't go anywhere near Gettysburg. I went there with my family and couldn't get out of the car."

I went on to tell her what else I saw: that she, then a male soldier, had survived the battle but was never the same. This past-life version of her lost his mind and eventually his whole family in the aftermath. So in this lifetime, family is very important to her. She laughed at this, and told me about the numerous events in her life this time around that came up about this theme of family, keeping her family intact, and making her family happy. When she connected this pattern in her current life and her experiences in a past life, something broke free. She left the event with resolve, knowing she would confront the depth of feeling she had around family with a little more softness.

When past lives are revealed to us, it is often for a reason like this. We each have thousands of past lives—more than we would ever be able to process. The purpose of them surfacing this way is to give us context for what we are experiencing in this life.

Our loved ones can sometimes show up to help with this process as well. On the Other Side, they can access even more information to help us contextualize what we are learning in this moment.

Phoenix has been with me throughout the writing of this book. I've felt his presence around me frequently. He's a good dog, and he represents companionship and support to me.

As I went about writing the second half of this book, I was regularly feeling a nervousness in the pit of my stomach. Usually, when I have this feeling, I know that I need to read somebody or do an energy release, but this time nothing revealed itself to me. It felt more spiritual than physical—it didn't seem like another symptom of menopause—so I chalked it up to anxiety about teaching my annual weekend workshop at Kripalu Center for Yoga & Health.

The feeling intensified as I finalized my plans for Kripalu. Finally, the weekend came around, and I taught my heart out, feeling the powerful channel move through me as I connected with the group. It was a special and fulfilling weekend, one that confirmed once again I am doing exactly what I came here to do. But on Sunday evening when the workshop was complete, the nervousness was still there. It was awful. It caught me completely off guard, and I was almost desperate to have the anxious churn in my belly release. *I miss my dog,* I thought, wishing I could run my fingers through his silky-soft fur.

When I woke up Monday morning, the feeling was still there. My Guides indicated I needed to go into an astral flight meditation—even though the thought of doing so exhausted me after having taught and channeled all weekend. But I knew I had to listen, so I closed the door of my room, sat up straight, and got to work.

First, one of my Guides arrived to accompany me. Then I felt myself moving through some dark passages, like hallways. Then I entered an open space. Shortly thereafter I got into some sort of vehicle and watched myself travel through trees backlit with golden light. After several minutes of this, I felt myself stop.

I heard the familiar scritch-scratch of Phoenix's nails. Then there he was, wagging his tail and wiggling all over, so excited to see me. My Guides had heard my prayer the night before! Shortly thereafter, other pets from throughout my life arrived, and I connected with them one by one. And then it was just me and Phoenix again. I hugged him and pressed my forehead to his.

That's when I heard it: ***Let go of the guilt.***

I felt guilt rush through and out of me—guilt I didn't even know I was carrying. I saw scenes from the end of Phoenix's life, during which I had wondered if I was making the right choice or cared for him well enough. And as I finally allowed myself to feel that guilt, someone appeared above him.

It was the spirit of my daughter. Not my daughter who is living today—the daughter I lost.

I heard it again: ***It's time to let go of the guilt.***

As I heard the words, I felt this guilt rush through me, too. It seemed both foreign and familiar, like a distant memory, like the guilt about Phoenix had felt just seconds before. It was separate from that guilt, and yet it was the same.

I've hesitated to write about this. It's a very vulnerable thing for me to share, and I know many people—perhaps even you, reading this right now—have lost pregnancies. Such a loss means different things to different people. It has different impacts. I don't want to push my experience onto yours.

But I think at some point, nearly every mother feels guilt for it. We wonder what we ate, what we did, what we thought that could have made it our fault. We wonder if we let our children down by grieving them too much or not enough. We wonder what we did wrong or if God hates us. Sometimes we may even twist spiritual truths to convince ourselves we're being punished. Losing a pregnancy—losing a child, a hope, a dream—comes with its own tangled mess of emotions. It's a knot of grief so complicated it transcends words. And in that moment, I finally let myself feel mine.

It took twenty-five years, but I got there. In that moment, in the loving presence of my Guides, my beloved dog, and the soul of the daughter who was never born, I felt my guilt move out and through me. I felt it release.

"For the highest and greatest good," I whispered through tears.

Slowly, I closed the meditation, offering gratitude for what I had experienced. I opened my eyes and looked at the clock. It was only 7:00 in the morning. What a way to start a day!

I got out my journal and began to process what I'd just experienced. Then at some point I put down my pen and asked aloud, "But seriously. Why now?"

Book.

It was just one word, but it made all the sense in the world to me. I've spent the last months talking about it and working through it and examining it. I've hashed it out with my editor and thought long and hard about how I want to present these ideas to you. And my Guides were not going to let me off easy—no way, not this time around. This lifetime is all about doing the work.

So here I am, doing mine, right along with you.

Putting It All Together

Who knows how many times I have experienced loss, guilt, and grief?

Who knows how many times I have felt like an impostor or not good enough? How many lifetimes have I spent comparing myself to others and falling short? How many lives were about learning, and unlearning, to people-please?

Who knows how many times I have struggled with instability, clinging to things in the material world to feel a sense of safety? Who knows how many times a home has been more than just shelter, but my whole sense of identity?

Who knows how many times I have dipped into these feelings without processing them completely, only to experience them once again as a second, third, fourth, or thousandth chance?

And who knows if I'm really done now? Not me. I have no idea—all I know is I'm a little bit closer.

The past affects the present, which affects the future. It goes around and around like that: through this lifetime and throughout many lifetimes. The question we have to ask ourselves is how often do I want to repeat these same lessons?

We'll meet up again and again in soul packs, going through the same feelings in different situations in an attempt to learn. We'll keep doing this until we're sufficiently tired of it all, until we don't want to fight anymore, until we are ready to learn whatever we need to learn, by doing whatever it takes, until we hold nothing back and give it our all. (And even then, maybe a little longer.)

Each one of us has to ask ourselves: Am I ready to free myself from this? *Really* ready? And if so, what am I willing to do, to sacrifice, to accept, in order to make that happen?

This is how we see things clearly. We stop looking at what is happening on the surface; we go a little deeper, then a little deeper still, until we reach the core of it all.

I've written extensively in these pages about our soul's plan. There are many people who believe that the plan, and all the experiences across lifetimes that accompany it, is actually accessible to us. As I mentioned previously, this idea is known as the ***Akashic Records***. By looking at these records, we can see past, present, and future, as well as how they are all connected.

Of course, these records are purely energetic. They exist beyond the structures of communication we have in this current manifestation of life. But because psychic input comes in through our existing frame of reference, we can envision these as we see fit. Some people see thousands of files on a giant computer. Others see a never-ending library of colorful, leather-bound books. You can envision it however you like—it's just a visual to help you understand. I often think of the records as unwritten, just balls of energy floating in space, waiting to be downloaded.

What if we could see these records? It's enough to know that they exist; the work can certainly be done with that information alone. But thinking of them helps me make sense of my own soul's plan and how it interacts with the plans of those around me. It helps me get to forgiveness and gratitude more quickly and easily, as I rise above my own worldly woes and see the big picture. It reminds me that this is all a learning process, a series of lessons my Guides wish to show me that form patterns that are uncomfortable precisely because my discomfort will force me to work with them.

In other words, it's my discomfort that will set me free. That is, if I'm willing to do the work.

We have to do the work. That's how we break the pattern. That's how we finish our contracts. We take full accountability for our actions in a way that is authentic and true to us. We turn directly toward what scares us, and we step on the gas.

To help you do this, I have two exercises for you. These are the last exercises in the book. I highly suggest you give them all you've got.

EXERCISE: PAST-LIFE REGRESSION

For this meditation, we're going to visit a past life. You may want a notebook and pen to write down what comes up.

It's important to note that not everyone will experience a past life in this meditation. Remember: rejection is protection! Sometimes Spirit doesn't show you things for a reason. If that happens, trust it! You can return to this meditation again another time.

Start by cleansing and grounding yourself. Then sit with your spine straight and your hands on your knees, palms facing up to receive. Breathe in and out a few times.

Then picture yourself at the age of twenty in this lifetime. If you're not twenty yet, then pick the age you are currently. See yourself—what you're wearing, how your hair is styled, where you are and what you are doing. Really study yourself.

Now move back to the age of ten. Really look at yourself.

Now see yourself at the age of five.

Feel the protection of your Guides all around you and see yourself in utero. See how you floated there inside your mother's womb.

Now picture yourself in a beautiful white room. You are wearing white from head to toe. One of your Guides is with you. Smile at them and thank them for being here. They are here to help.

Look to the far end of the room to spot a door labeled "past life." Walk toward that door, breathing deeply, feeling relaxed.

On the other side of this door is one of your past lives. The one you will see is the one that is most relatable to your life in this moment—the one that will show you things about the challenges you face today. When you're ready, let your Guide lead you through the door.

Now you are on the other side of the door in your past life. Take a look at your surroundings. What are you wearing? Where do you think you are? Allow your Guide to fill in any blanks in your vision as you gather as much information from this lifetime as you can.

When you're ready, walk back through the door into the beautiful white room.

Take a moment to look around the room until you see a new door labeled "present life."

On the other side of this door is the circumstance in this lifetime that the previous lifetime, the one you just saw, is here to help you understand. When you're ready, let your Guide lead you through the door.

Now you are on the other side of the door in your current lifetime, seeing how your past-life experience relates to the challenges you face today. What can you learn and understand based on what you are seeing? Do you have more space for compassion? For gratitude? For forgiveness? Allow the lesson or lessons to seep into the core of your being. If your Guide has anything to add, let them speak it aloud or show it to you.

When you are ready, walk back through the door into the beautiful white room. Turn and see it close behind you. Now look to your Guide and thank them for accompanying you today and for revealing what they showed you.

Take a few deep breaths and come back into your body. Open your eyes. You may wish to write about your experience.

BONUS EXERCISE: ACCESS THE AKASHIC RECORDS

For this meditation, we will visit the Akashic Records. These will appear to you in a way that is comfortable and makes sense based on your frame of reference, so let your imagination go wild! Remember that it is all energy just presenting itself to you in a way you can understand. If you weave memories, pop culture references, etc., into your understanding of your library and librarian, you're doing it exactly right!

It's important that you pay attention to any numbers, symbols, images, names, and other small details that arise. You'll want a journal and a pen to write down what you experience, as well as to take note of any of these small details. Even if they don't make sense to you now, their meaning may be revealed in the coming days.

While the Akashic Records hold anything and everything that could ever be known about anything and everything in the Universe, today we're going to focus on the small part of this library that is personal to you. The information in this part pertains to your individual soul and the lessons it is learning throughout its incarnations.

Accessing the Akashic Records is an advanced practice. It is meant for those who have done a good deal of work already and are prepared to receive more information about their soul's plan. It's a sacred practice, and one I recommend doing sparingly. As you reach the end of this book, you are in the perfect place to be shown deep and important truths about your incarnation. Your Guides will support you in this.

To begin the meditation, start by cleansing and grounding yourself. Then sit with your spine straight and your hands on your knees, palms facing up. Close your eyes and take a few deep breaths to settle into this position and clear your mind. Connect with your spiritual self and gently set your physical body aside. Do this by visualizing yourself being filled with radiant white light and imagining your spiritual self gently lifting and moving away from your physical form.

Now, envision a hallway in front of you. You can make it look as ornate or as simple as you like. The hallway is lined with doors on both sides.

At the end of the hallway, straight in front of you, is a door. Ask a Guide to join you, and when you feel them arrive, walk toward that door together.

As you walk, feel the color red wash over you. Keep walking and feel the red turn to orange. Keep walking as orange becomes yellow, encompassing your entire being. Keep walking toward the door as yellow turns to green. Keep walking as you are engulfed in blue. You are almost to the door when blue turns to indigo. And now, as you stand in front of the door with your Guide at your side, you are bathed in a brilliant white light that surrounds you and reaches all the way through your body. Note if you see any numbers or symbols on the door, and pay attention to its detail. Look for the handle of the door: Is it a knob? A lever? A chain? Feel this white light around and within you as you reach for the door handle.

Now, open the door and walk through it, with your Guide following you for support.

On the other side of the door the first thing you see is your librarian. Take a good look at them, however they appear. Do you recognize them? Is something about them familiar? Does the way the librarian has presented themself to you bring up any emotions or memories? Notice this without judging them or yourself.

Now, ask your librarian to take you and your Guide to your books. Look up and see all the books lining the walls of this space, reaching up and down into infinity. Allow your librarian to pull three books down and present them to you on a table.

On the cover of one of the books it says, "Past." On the second book it says, "Present." On the third book it says, "Future."

When you are ready, with your Guide supporting you at your side and with the assistance of your librarian, open the "Past" book. Take a moment to understand what it is showing you.

When you are complete, close this book and open the "Present" book. Absorb the message for you there.

When you are complete, close this book and open the "Future" book. Allow this information to permeate your being.

When you are complete with all three books, thank your librarian for showing you these things and thank your Guide for supporting you. Turn and see the door behind you once again. Walk through it into the hall, into the brilliant white light.

Far ahead of you at the other end of the hall, see the room where your body is now sitting. Begin to walk toward it, passing doorways on your left and right. Walk as the white light turns to indigo. Then feel it turn blue. Keep walking as it turns green, then yellow, then orange. When it turns red, you are nearly at the end of the hallway. Then reenter your body.

Take a few deep breaths in this space and open your eyes.

Open your journal and write as much as you can about this experience. The Akashic Records show everything there is to know. Trust that they have picked the most important and pertinent tidbits for you to experience today. Write down anything you understand about what you were shown, as well as any questions you still have about the meaning of what you saw. These questions will be answered over the coming days.

CONCLUSION
TAKE THE SCENIC ROUTE

WE HAVE REACHED THE END OF OUR STRETCH TOGETHER—AT least, we have for now.

Let's look back on the road we've traveled.

As we began to comprehend what Spirit Guides are and the role they play in our lives, we expanded our understanding of how they can communicate with us. We embraced the idea of an unknown destination, welcoming the open road and all it has to offer. By making peace with our loved ones and our past, we opened up even more space for the journey. We then considered divine timing and the role of patience—and impatience—along the way.

As our practices became more advanced, we looked at mixed messages and roadblocks, learning how to deal with both with creativity and good humor. We then explored the role of our not-so-savory emotions. To further our understanding, we took a closer look at the lessons our souls incarnated to learn and the supreme importance of taking accountability for our role in learning those lessons enthusiastically. Finally, we considered the grand scheme of things, understanding on an even deeper level that our work is never done. We are always learning, always finding our way, and that is precisely how it is supposed to be!

In the process, I have done my very best to lead you through this work without giving you any false impressions. I'm just another human being who has come here to learn my lessons. I encourage you to take what serves you and leave the rest behind. Spice it up however you like. Follow your own guidance, and make your own way. I trust in your Guides—as should you!—and know that they will lead you down the road that is right for you.

You are always the one in the driver's seat. The way you choose to look at your life and your lessons is completely up to you, as is what you choose to manifest and put out into the world. It is my humble suggestion that you do so joyfully, in a way that is authentic to you without worrying about what anyone else thinks—including me.

Give yourself permission to live your best life with your Guides at your side. This is the lifetime in which you are ready to look at your challenges as opportunities. Your Guides are here to help you do this, because when you work with them, you're working with your higher self to write your best and truest story. You're building the road as you travel it with confidence and grace. My final wish for you is this clarity of vision. May your life be everything you ever dreamed—and more.

Go ahead, take the scenic route! Enjoy it. Every bit of this journey is meant for you.

ACKNOWLEDGMENTS

A deep thank you to the amazing souls in my life both here and there. . . .

To Chandika. Thank you. Once again you have helped me share the words that Spirit has given me to serve. I am so thankful for our time together, for your incredible talent and for the love and energy that you gave to this book. Thank you too for talking me through sharing my stories. I couldn't have done it without you.

To my beautiful soul sister Gabby Bernstein. Thank you for your friendship, your sisterhood and your unwavering support. I cherish our relationship. You are the true representation of "there is room for all."

To my incredible earthly team of lightworkers at Team MaryAnn! Thank you! I am so grateful for all that you do for me. I appreciate each one of you. You are valued and you are loved by me. Cheers to more growth, fun road trips, and lots of sourdough bread!

To my agent Michele Martin. You are a force! Thank you for challenging me to do my best, for your honesty, and for your dedication and support through every step of our projects together.

To Jaspre Guest and her fabulous PR team. I am so grateful for all your support and enthusiasm for this book. You all go above and beyond, and I am once again thrilled to have you by my side. LFG!

To my editor Shannon Fabricant and the wonderful team at Running Press, thank you so much for believing in this book and in me! Working together has been a lovely experience, full of light and love.

To Pat Longo and my amazing psychic friends, who have remained close to me all these years. Thank you for your love and support. For sharing your stories, lessons and messages. 11:11.

To my dear friend and fellow Pisces Kristen Bly. Words alone cannot describe the gratitude I have in my heart for our friendship. Our coffee talks are some of my most cherished moments. Thank you for all that you give to our relationship. Love you so much!

To my dear NoFo friends, you are all a forever constant in my life. No matter where I am or what I am going through, I know you have my back and I will always have yours! I love you all!

To my sweet bestie in life Corinne. You have seen me through some of my darkest hours and have been a champion of my joy. I am so grateful for your love and support. We are family. You are my sister. Forever.

To my brother Anthony. Spirit has taken us into a new chapter of our relationship, and I couldn't be more thrilled. I am so proud of you! Thank you for your love and guidance.

To my family, my parents, and my sister. Thank you for loving me unconditionally. Thank you too for your patience and understanding while my life has grown and changed. Our time together has created beautiful memories that hold space in the happiest places of my heart.

To my beautiful children. May you continue to manifest your dreams, embody happiness, and bask in all that this amazing world has to give. Love you so much.

To my husband. Chris, my soul has known and loved you lifetime after lifetime. Thank you for all that you do for us and our family. There is no one I would rather walk through life with. Always. All ways.

To my incredible students, thank you for your trust. I have loved working with each one of you. As I teach, I continue to learn. You have shared your lives with me and have allowed Spirit to guide us along the way. I am so proud of all of you!

To Source, my Spirit Guides, loved ones, and angels who have been ever present in my life. I am humbled by all that you have guided me to. Thank you for providing me with the energy and the words to serve.

INDEX

RAISING READERS

Books Build Bright Futures

Thank you for reading this book and for being a reader of books in general. As an author, I am so grateful to share being part of a community of readers with you, and I hope you will join me in passing our love of books on to the next generation of readers.

Did you know that reading for enjoyment is the single biggest predictor of a child's future happiness and success?

More than family circumstances, parents' educational background, or income, reading impacts a child's future academic performance, emotional well-being, communication skills, economic security, ambition, and happiness.

Studies show that kids reading for enjoyment in the US is in rapid decline:

- In 2012, 53% of 9-year-olds read almost every day. Just 10 years later, in 2022, the number had fallen to 39%.
- In 2012, 27% of 13-year-olds read for fun daily. By 2023, that number was just 14%.

Together, we can commit to **Raising Readers** and change this trend. How?

- Read to children in your life daily.
- Model reading as a fun activity.
- Reduce screen time.
- Start a family, school, or community book club.
- Visit bookstores and libraries regularly.
- Listen to audiobooks.
- Read the book before you see the movie.
- Encourage your child to read aloud to a pet or stuffed animal.
- Give books as gifts.
- Donate books to families and communities in need.

Books build bright futures, and **Raising Readers** is our shared responsibility.

For more information, visit **JoinRaisingReaders.com**

Sources: National Endowment for the Arts, National Assessment of Educational Progress, WorldBookDay.org, Nielsen BookData's 2023 "Understanding the Children's Book Consumer"

BOB1217